1/93

CONTEMPORARY
ARGENTINE
CINEMA

CONTEMPORARY ARGENTINE CINEMA

DAVID WILLIAM FOSTER

UNIVERSITY OF MISSOURI PRESS

COLUMBIA AND LONDON

Library of Congress Cataloging-in-Publication Data

Foster, David William.
    Contemporary Argentine cinema / David William Foster.
        p.   cm.
    Includes bibliographical references and index.
    ISBN 0-8262-0860-6 (alk. paper)
    1. Motion pictures—Argentina.   2. Motion pictures—Political
aspects—Argentina.   3. Motion pictures—Social aspects—Argentina.
I. Title.
PN1993.5.A7F6   1992
791.43'0982—dc20   92-27908
                                                                    CIP

∞™ This paper meets the requirements of the
American National Standard for Permanence of Paper
for Printed Library Materials, Z39.48, 1984.

Designer: Elizabeth K. Fett
Typesetter: Connell-Zeko Type & Graphics
Printer and binder: Thomson-Shore, Inc.
Typeface: Garamond Book

Para Virginia y David Raúl

CONTENTS

■ ■ ■ ■ ■ ACKNOWLEDGMENTS ■ ■ ■ ■ ■

The research for this study was made possible by various grant programs of Arizona State University and by the collaborative contributions of my research assistants, Roselyn Costantino, Gustavo Geirola, Darrell B. Lockhart, and Manuel Murrieta, and the editorial assistance of Katharine Kaiper Phillips. Naomi Lindstrom made valuable comments on the final draft of the manuscript. Various individuals in Argentina facilitated my access to films: Elida B. Messina, Enrique Medina, and Teo Kofman. This project, like other studies on Argentine culture during and following military tyranny, is part of a dialogue that I have had the good fortune to maintain with individuals from many sectors of Argentine society over a period of twenty-five years, a period that included all the military dictatorships between 1967 and 1983 and also the return to democracy.

The following individuals have graciously provided authorization to include in this study illustrative material: Raúl Tosso (*Gerónima*); Héctor Olivera (*No habrá más penas ni olvido*); Lita Stantic (*Camila*); Argentina Sono Films (*Sur* and *Tangos: el exilio de Gardel*); Cinequanon Films (*Hombre mirando al sudeste*).

CONTEMPORARY
ARGENTINE
CINEMA

■ ■ ■ ■ ■ INTRODUCTION ■ ■ ■ ■ ■

In 1983 Argentina returned to constitutional democracy after a decade of military dictatorship. The process of redemocratization, officially sponsored by the new government and pursued vigorously throughout public and private sectors of the cultural establishment, brought with it an enormous renewed cultural production.[1] Traditional cultural forms like literary and general interest magazines, novels, and dramatic works constituted a particularly extensive part of this production.[2] Television programming was expanded to include not only enhanced national productions but also productions that echoed the goals of redemocratization. It augmented coverage of contemporary sociopolitical issues and contributed to the analysis of the devastating consequences for national life of the military government, including the "dirty war" against alleged subversives and the lamentable Malvinas (Falkland Islands) operation.[3]

One of the areas of cultural production that received special attention was filmmaking.[4] As B. Ruby Rich has observed: "The 1980s were a time for optimism regarding the revision and reinvention of the New Latin American Cinema in a contemporary guise. The breaking of taboo and prohibition, the freeing of the imagination to fantasy, a respect for the mundane and everyday,

1. Basic position statements include Marcos Aguinis, *Mientras se consolida la democracia;* Javier Torre and Adriana Zaffaroni, "Argentina: Its Culture during the Repression and during the Transition"; and Oscar Landi, "Campo cultural y democratización en Argentina."

2. See, for example, the cultural products analyzed by Aníbal Ford, Jorge B. Rivera, and Eduardo Romano, *Medios de comunicación y cultura popular.*

3. See Aguinis, *Mientras se consolida la democracia;* Mónica Peralta-Ramos and Carlos H. Waisman, eds., *From Military Rule to Liberal Democracy;* and *Hacia una Argentina posible.*

4. Peter B. Schumann, *Historia del cine latinoamericano,* 38–51; John King and Nissa Torrents, eds., *The Garden of Forking Paths: Argentine Cinema,* 74–97.

1

the introduction of humor and music, the construction of new narrative strategies, and the reconsideration of the relationship to the audience, have all contributed to what I've defined as the monumental task of forging a new 'collective subjectivity.' "[5] Argentina had a long tradition of commercial and art films dating from the earliest days of the industry in the late nineteenth and early twentieth centuries.[6] Numerous Argentine directors attained international recognition, and many Argentine film people have pursued their careers in the United States (Lalo Schifrin in soundtrack music and the actress Norma Aleandro are only two recent examples). Through the Instituto Argentino de Cinematografía, the elected government that assumed power in late 1983 undertook to promote its policies of redemocratization through the stimulation of film production. During the following five years, several dozen major Argentine films, in one way or another, explored sociopolitical themes brought to the fore by redemocratization and the analysis of recent Argentine history. By 1988 economic problems began seriously to curtail film production underwritten by the Instituto— problems that were exacerbated by the fact that few of the films it underwrote were big money-makers, having to contend during the postcensorship era with the flood of foreign imports, always more appealing to an Argentine audience than Argentine or other Latin American films.[7]

Some of the Argentine films, however, notably Luis Puenzo's *La historia oficial* (The official story), which won the 1986 Oscar for the best foreign film, attracted international attention and had wide distribution in the United States and Europe, being readily available in video stores. Puenzo's film is, in large measure, emblematic of the renewed cultural production. Films like *Camila*

5. B. Ruby Rich, "An/Other View of New Latin American Cinema," 23.

6. *Historia del cine argentino;* Agustín Mahieu, *Breve historia del cine nacional;* Jorge A. Schnitman, *Film Industries in Latin America: Dependency and Development;* and Schumann, *Historia del cine latinoamericano.*

7. One dimension of economic circumstances in Argentina, alongside the rise of video clubs and home viewing, was the drastic reduction in the number of movie houses. According to statistics released by the Sindicato de la Industria Cinematográfica Argentina, in 1970 there were over 2,000 movie houses in Argentina; by the 1980–1982 period, the number had dropped to 900; in October, 1991, there were 427; and in January, 1992, there were approximately 380 (Teo Kofman, private communication based on documents in his possession).

(filmed by Argentina's most prominent woman director, María Luisa Bemberg), Eliseo Subiela's *Hombre mirando al sudeste* (Man facing southeast), and Fernando Solanas's *Tango, el exilio de Gardel* (Tango, the exile of Gardel) are all outstanding examples of films produced with a high degree of technical skill and commercial gloss while at the same time addressing in a conscientious fashion the sociopolitical issues. These films are accompanied by others that may not have received the same degree of public acclaim but that, nevertheless, also demonstrate the new vitality in Argentine filmmaking during the second half of the 1980s: Pablo César's *La sagrada familia* (The holy family), Raúl A. Tosso's *Gerónima,* Teo Kofman's *Perros de la noche* (The dogs of night), Américo Ortiz de Zárate's *Otra historia de amor* (Another love story), and María Luisa Bemberg's *Miss Mary,* to name only the most prominent.

This study undertakes a detailed analysis of the intersection in these films between the strategies of commercial filmmaking and the project of Argentine redemocratization, building on the important research area of film and society in Latin America and the so-called Third World.[8] The study examines the material chosen for filming, the technical decisions made in the process of filming, and the organizing ideological voice that provides each film with its structural coherence. Of interest is a consideration of the overall thematic nature of each film, the sort of social world it projects, and the types of spectators and spectator response it implies. Special emphasis is placed on the narrative pattern of each film—the ways in which action is framed, the connectives that link the various scenes, the relationship between primary and secondary characters, the use of highlighting and foregrounding—as a key to its interpretation of individual and collective sociopolitical experience in Argentina. The analysis also seeks to determine what implications derive from the fact that the films were made both for Argentine and for international consumption and therefore need to encode information about Argentine history that foreign audiences are not likely to possess. Finally, since all of these elements involve complex semiotic processes, special attention centers on

8. "El cine en América Latina"; Teshome H. Gabriel, *Third Cinema in the Third World: The Aesthetics of Liberation;* E. Bradford Burns, *Latin American Cinema: Film and History;* and Roy Armes, *Third World Film Making and the West.*

the ideological complications that arise from the cinematographic configuration of social meaning in contemporary Argentina.

Since this study pretends to go beyond the circumscribed, intrinsic analysis of film style and structure in order to examine a block of cinema productions as ideological texts, it is necessary to engage in a series of considerations concerning the relationships between film and society that inform the following chapters. Teshome Gabriel offers the following principles for the study of what has come to be called the Third Cinema, or filmmaking in the Third World that rejects the traditional Hollywood view of films as mass-distributed and commercially profitable entertainment:

> The infant study of Third Cinema has already set as its point of departure the examination of the unique context—cultural and ideological—in which these films have been produced. The critical inquiry that has evolved must address jointly the areas of text and context and it is to that end that the following should be taken into account.
>
> Third Cinema must, above all, be recognized as a cinema of subversion. It is a cinema that emerges from the peoples who have suffered under the spells of mystified cinema and who seek the demystification of representational practices as part of the process of liberation. Third Cinema aims at a destruction and construction at the same time: a destruction of the images of colonial or neo-colonial cinema, and a construction of another cinema that captures the revolutionary impulse of the peoples of the Third World. It is a progressive cinema founded on folk culture whose role it is to intervene on behalf of the peoples of Africa, Asia and Latin America who must fight equally for political as well as cultural liberation.
>
> A critical examination of Third Cinema cannot take place outside of a comprehensive knowledge of the lives and struggles of Third World people, in both their past and their present histories. Lacking this historical perspective, the film critic or theorist can only reflect on the ways in which this cinema undermines and innovates traditional practices of representation, but he/she will lose sight of the context in which the cinema operates. An equally significant component of the critical perspective that must be adopted is the recognition of the TEXT that pre-exists each new text and that binds the filmmaker to a set of values, mores, traditions and behaviors—in a word, "culture"—which is at all moments the obligatory point of departure. Without the necessary understanding of this pre-existent TEXT, critical inquiry would fall into the trap of auteurist fallacies and "aesthetic" evaluative stances.[9]

There are several problems in extending Gabriel's position to the

9. Gabriel, *Third Cinema in the Third World,* 95.

Argentine filmmaking of the period of redemocratization. Aside from the dangers inherent in sustaining a global notion like the Third World, no matter what validity it has Argentina is hardly a Third World country in the way that, say, Bolivia is. And although it may be argued that Argentina, beyond the Avenida General Paz that separates the federal capital from the rest of the country, does present persuasive continuities with the Third World, Buenos Aires, at least in its culture-generating and culture-consuming nucleus, is not only non–Third World but aggressively anti–Third World. This circumstance cannot fail to have implications for the sort of films to be produced in Argentina by even the most socially committed of directors. Gabriel speaks of the use of folklore motifs as a confirming characteristic of Third Cinema, which implies a disjunction with the Eurocentrist trappings notable in commercial productions. Such trappings provide images of actual spheres of Latin American modernity or facets of a wish fantasy that is assumed to be alluring to mass audiences. While some Argentine filmmaking has made use of that country's rich folkloric traditions and has sought to portray human lives lived in accordance with world-views other than those promoted by the Porteño cultural establishment, directors have not generally viewed the folkloric as the site of alternate social realities.[10] Both the urban lumpen and the rural margins tend to be viewed as clinging to little more than vestiges of the capitalist promise.

Fernando Birri, a legendary Argentine director who has lived in recent decades in Cuba, expresses a position that may have greater resonance for Argentine efforts.

WHAT KIND OF CINEMA DOES ARGENTINA NEED? WHAT KIND OF CINEMA DO THE UNDERDEVELOPED PEOPLE OF LATIN AMERICA NEED?
A cinema which develops them.
    A cinema which brings them consciousness, which awakens consciousness; which clarifies matters; which strengthens the revolutionary consciousness of those among them who already possess this; which fires them; which disturbs, worries, shocks and weakens those who have a "bad conscience," a reactionary consciousness; which defines profiles of national, Latin American identity; which is authentic; which

---

10. *Porteño* refers to the cultural establishment of Buenos Aires, an international port city.

is anti-oligarchic and anti-bourgeois at the national level, and anti-colonial and anti-imperialist at the international level; which is pro-people, and anti-anti-people; which helps the passage from underdevelopment to development, from sub-stomach to stomach, from sub-culture to culture, from sub-happiness to happiness, from sub-life to life.

Our purpose is to create a new person, a new society, a new history and therefore a new art and a new cinema. Urgently.[11]

While there is still much of the Cuban-centered Third World rhetoric about Birri's statements, a rhetoric not easily subscribed to by sophisticated Buenos Aires cultural spokespersons, it is nevertheless quite evident that there are clear correspondences between the position from which Birri is writing—the need for a thoroughgoing social revolution—and the process of redemocratization in Argentina. The latter was not committed, at either an official or popular level, to revolution in the socialist sense underlying Birri's words. But the need to repudiate fascism and military rule, the need to reconstruct Argentine society and its culture along meaningfully democratic lines, and the imperative to offer cultural texts that would, in noncommercial and nonexploitative ways, contribute to the new social and historical consciousness of "never again" were determining factors in the cinematographic production being spoken of here. (*Nunca mas* [Never again] was the title of the official government report on the disappeared.)

Moviemaking in Argentina in the postmilitary period undoubtedly demonstrated a more pronounced break with the past than did other forms of cultural production. Literature offered a sustained model of cultural resistance during the tyranny, as did some manifestations of popular music, popular art (like the magazine *Humor Registrado* [Registered humor]), and other print media.[12] The theater also included significant works of a subversive nature; the Teatro Abierto (Open theater) movement begun in 1981 represented such a loudly defiant voice of cultural resistance that it became a symbol of the defiance of censorship and repression at a time when military authority had already begun to weaken.[13] But movies, along with television, because of the large capital investment required for production and distribution and their enormous

11. Fernando Birri, "Cinema and Underdevelopment," 9.
12. For example, the papers included in *Ficción y política: la narrativa argentina durante el proceso militar,* edited by Beatriz Sarlo.
13. Carlos Ferreira, *Por un cine libre.*

public visibility, were severely circumscribed during the Proceso de Reorganización Nacional (Process of National Reorganization), the name given by the military to the political programs it put into effect after the 1976 coup.

Although some innovative work with sociopolitical implications was done outside Argentina by Argentine directors (for example, Héctor Babenco in Brazil), film production in Argentina was almost exclusively in the Hollywood mold—or, at least, films were produced that could in no way pose a threat to the regime. Television programming relied heavily on dubbed foreign, mostly American, syndications, with only some innocuous national productions.[14] Seditious films were accessible through several underground means: importation and viewing of cassettes of banned movies by small circles; private screenings, ostensibly for publicity purposes, of films, including some countercultural Latin American items that could not be publicly released without cuts by the censors; and word-of-mouth or ciphered interpretations of commercially available foreign films, with or without cuts. The latter could contribute allegorical readings of Argentina's current political situation, either because they confirmed the structures of fascism or because they could be argued to insinuate an opposition to it, if only a timid and perhaps contradictory one.

Thus the filmmaking that gathered momentum in Argentina after the return to democracy constituted a newly defined cultural component, whereas other cultural products only increased the quantity of their texts and the openness of sociopolitical themes. In this sense, film production was more closely coterminous with the process of redemocratization than were other cultural manifestations, lending it a greater symbolic aura and, because of its potential for mass consumption in ways that literature and the theater lack, allowing it a heightened internal and foreign distribution. Outside Argentina, the films produced after 1983 and throughout the rest of the decade have been widely accepted as indexes of that country's transcendence of military rule.

For President Raúl Alfonsín's government and the various permanent and ad hoc agencies involved in cultural production, cul-

---

14. Heriberto Muraro, and José G. Cantor Magnani, "La influencia transnacional en el cine argentino."

ture was to play a key role in the process of redemocratization. This was natural, since the military, hardly underestimating, if not really understanding, the role of culture in society, had done much to destroy coherent cultural practices. Indeed, culture in Argentina had been besieged, with only brief respites in the late 1950s and early 1960s and in 1973, by all manner of military interventions since 1930, when a fascist coup installed José Félix Uriburu. As a consequence, redemocratization meant not just opposition to the dictatorship between 1976 and 1983 but, more significantly, the forging of a new institutionalism within the context of several generations of repeated aggressions—culture not only restored but an integral component of national consciousness.

Film deserved to be supported; Argentina could rightfully be proud of its historical leadership in Latin America in all aspects of filmmaking. The infrastructure of an industry was already in place and overlapped with the Buenos Aires theater world, still the driving force in Latin America, and with television, one of the largest enterprises on the continent and the first with color installations (thanks to the dictatorship's use of the 1978 World Soccer Cup in Argentina as a propaganda tool). Moreover, with regard to mass-distribution possibilities, not only did Buenos Aires enjoy a vast infrastructure for the showing of films, but films often appealed to an international audience in ways that few other cultural products could. Finally, and perhaps most important, film offered an all-enveloping illusion of reality far greater than television, the theater, or literature. Certainly, this illusion is fraught with ideological traps and allows precisely for the sort of manipulation of the spectator that is considered to be the worst aspect of commercial filmmaking. Yet this illusionism allowed for a greater immediacy for images of sociopolitical reality and for a complex set of signs that could eloquently bring into play critical attitudes and revisionist/ revolutionary modelings that were essential to reconfiguring the national consciousness as part of the process of democratization.

It will remain an open question whether this filmmaking—or, better, specific texts—should be viewed as modernist or postmodernist, as experimental or conservative.[15] The fact that these films

15. D. N. Rodowick, *The Crisis of Political Modernism: Criticism and Ideology in Contemporary Film Theory.*

essentially aspired to an appraisal of a well-defined sociopolitical reality—Argentina during the military tyranny and Argentina during the period of redemocratization—means that the self-reflective and distancing procedures associated with experimental productions are inappropriate here. Moreover, modernist versus postmodernist postures are fundamentally bypassed, even when it is possible to talk about sophisticated spectator preferences that may condition response to certain texts. For example, postmodernist enthusiasms in Buenos Aires may have had much to do with a goodly amount of disdain for most of the films discussed in this study; individuals culturally raised at the movies viewed them as too transparent and ideologically naive, as technically clumsy, and as insufficiently engaged with the issues of a *cinéma internationale* to merit more than passing attention.

But, then, it is extremely dangerous to speak in generalities about an Argentine or a Porteño movie audience. There exist no published sociological or market studies about who goes to the movies in Argentina, and hence it is difficult to speak in anything other than impressionistic terms about audience values, expectations, interpretive horizons, and the like. The reading of literature is a solitary act, and so we understand that literary criticism, no matter what level of complexity it assumes, is inescapably one person's reaction to a text. But the movies continue to be public spectacles, and even the home viewing of video cassettes tends to be done in a group. Yet film criticism, like any criticism other than a sociological survey of responses, is also a solitary analysis, a personal opinion.

But what seems to be more of a problem in the analysis of film vis-à-vis the spectator in Argentina is less a question of audience reaction in either personal or collective terms than of public preferences for foreign films. This preference was enhanced in the post–1983 period by the decensorship of imports; films were no longer banned or subjected to often confusing cuts, and there even arose a small but nevertheless significant exhibition of pornographic movies. The fact that audiences had access to so many movies that had never been shown in Argentina and to complete versions of movies that had been shown with cuts only served to increase the competition between Argentine movies and foreign imports. As usual, American titles were abundant, but more significant was the considerable representation of key European films that had never passed the censors. The competition was further accentuated by the emergence of the home video industry. Video agencies and clubs seemed to have sprung up on every street corner, and their holdings were almost exclusively Hollywood productions, dubbed or subtitled. (One still visits them in vain looking for Argentine or Latin American films, which may be rented or bought only after extreme perseverance. This assertion is based on personal experiences in gathering copies of the films included in this study.) The result was that as production costs and ticket prices soared with inflation and the decline of the dollar in the late 1980s, the reemergent Argentine film industry also experienced heavy and, in the end, fatal competition from an industry whose profits were based virtually exclusively on the attraction of foreign imports.

While Argentine directors between 1983 and the end of the decade did not invest heavily in experimental cinematography, it is unquestionable that they did strive to stand in opposition to the commercial Hollywood norm and to make use of some of the principles of modernist and postmodernist filmmaking, or what D. N. Rodowick calls "counter-cinema."

> [T]he reflexive structure of the text of political modernism is mapped onto a series of formal negations organized according to the opposition of modernism to realism. In this respect, the text of countercinema is marked by its interiorization and critical interrogation of the codes of Hollywood narrative cinema—for example, narrative transitivity (linear and teleological exposition); emotional identification with the characters and diegesis; representational transparency (masking of the means of production); a singular, unified, and homogenous diegetic space; textual closure presupposing a self-contained fiction— all of which are designed to yield a narrative pleasure aimed at pacifying the spectator.
>   In point of fact, . . . counter-cinema, which must accomplish the semiotic "deconstruction" of these elements of code, may be described in three points.
>   1. The text of political modernism cannot be conceived instrumental. . . .
>   2. Once the text has been opened up centrifugally—that is, once it has become intertextual—a difficulty in reading is imposed. . . .
>   3. This practice of reading imposed by the form of the modernist text generates a subjective response [called] "meaning effects."[16]

16. Ibid., 52–54.

Surely, there is much about the Argentine production under consideration that exploits the narrativity of the Hollywood film, especially when critical or uncritical intertextualities appear together with the conventions of soap opera, as in Puenzo's *The Official Story* or Ortiz de Zárate's *Another Love Story*. Perhaps only Solanas's *Tango, the Exile of Gardel* and *Sur* (South side) are unstintingly modernist, along with certain aspects of Subiela's science-fiction *Man Facing Southeast*. Yet all are marked by the sign of political modernism in the imperative to stimulate critical attitudes on the part of the spectator and to counteract the tradition of pacification Rodowick identifies as an essential component of the Hollywood mode—pacification in the sense of accepting reality as it is judged to be and refusing to entertain any ideological-dialectical critique of history. Perhaps few of the formulations are specifically Marxian, but the questioning of history, understood either in its conventional accumulated-past sense or as the Marxist here-and-now, is a unifying thread of the Argentine process of redemocratization, and it is in this sense that these films stand in opposition to the bulk of the commercial imports.

A number of recurring features of the films examined herein are characteristic of the resistance to narrative readability and the promotion of a critical and self-reflective countercinema of the type that Rodowick describes. One such feature is an appeal to allegorical configurations. While *allegory,* like so many of the conceptual terms used in literary criticism and extended to film analysis, is often overly flexible in its applications, the use of it here means to refer to the way in which characters, places, situations, and events have a historical meaning beyond their immediate, personal signification. A transparent semiosis implies that nothing has any meaning beyond itself and that, as a consequence, no story has any transcendent meaning beyond the trivially circumstantial, the essence of escapist meaning. Allegory, however, directs the spectator to understand how the personal is political and how the particular is historical, because every element in the social fabric is an interwoven part of the whole. In *The Official Story,* Gaby *is* Gaby as part of an intensely personal world, but she is also a sign for the destruction of innocence by military tyranny through the violent manipulation of individual destinies. Gaby's particular story is also the story of expanding spheres of Argentine social life, and spectator anxiety over her uncertain future at the end of the film points also toward the unresolved dilemmas of national existence. The repression of Rantes in Subiela's *Man Facing Southeast* and the persecutions of the gay lovers in *Another Love Story* are intrinsic to a set of personal lives, but both repression and persecution are constituents of a social dynamic the respective films are concerned to elucidate.

Documentalism is another sustained characteristic of the films of the Argentine period of redemocratization. Documentary, in either a literal sense or in the sense of the documentary-like re-creation of events from an earlier era, is an important form of contemporary filmmaking, and there are a number of Argentine monuments in this genre, such as Fernando Solanas's *La hora de los hornos* (The hour of the furnaces), Octavio Getino and Solanas's *La Patagonia rebelde* (Rebellious Patagonia), Héctor Olivera's *Los hijos de Fierro* (The sons of Fierro), and Eduardo Mignogna's *Evita, quien quiera oír, que oiga* (Evita, let he who wants to, listen). Documentary films, however, engage in a number of strategies to ensure audience recognition of the fact that fictional elements, if present at all, are only adjuncts to a core of archival material presented via a filmic exposition. Documentalism, by contrast, incorporates into a fictional narrative archival material as part of the expository texture of the narrative: the actual footage in *The Official Story* of the Madres de Plaza de Mayo (Mothers of Mayo Plaza) marching, veristic images of urban slums in Kofman's *The Dogs of Night,* television journalism footage in Bebe Kamín's *Los chicos de la guerra* (The boys of the war).

Documentalism serves to anchor a narrative in a specific sociopolitical reality in order to trigger allegorical associations in the spectators' interpretation of a film. Cultural texts create an illusion of reality, beginning with the use of sign entities identified as human characters, while often at the same time reflecting facile decodifications of fictional reality as being merely transparent images of real life. Real life, of course, is not what takes place in cultural texts, at least not as such, although films (like television dramas) are particularly susceptible to being taken as open windows on actual life. Cultural texts, rather, are semiotic reconfigurations of real life, and the sense of meaning they propagate allows signs to posit a denser, overdetermined signification that the haphazard, random, and essentially infinite components of lived experience cannot have. Cultural texts expropriate signs from the latter and conscientiously structure them so that they will enter into processes of meaning spectators can contemplate or extrapolate in a manner specifically focused by the cultural event, or the entire ceremony associated with seeing a movie and deriving something from it. Cultural texts mediate and thereby defer real life, and yet documentalism and the overall appeal to verisimilitude in many cultural texts function to anchor the texts in recognizable social and historical realities. Argentine post–1983 films are historical in any sense of the adjective, and documentalism is one way of enhancing continuities with acknowledged historical material.

History in the conventional sense of an accumulated past is also a component of these films, the most notable example being Bemberg's *Camila,* which is based on an actual event from the mid-nineteenth century. The implication is that the structure of repression and tyranny of that period prefigures recent Argentine history, and the film is both historically accurate in its details and anachronistic in the foreshadowing of contemporary reenactments of bloody narrative programs.

Postmodernist deconstructive recodifications of science fiction in *Man Facing Southeast,* of Nazi propaganda films in Héctor Babenco's *Kiss of the Spider Woman,* of the soap opera in *Another Love Story,* and of pornographic erotica in *The Dogs of Night* represent yet another dimension of turning transparent narrativity into analytical countercinema without aspiring to an uncompromisingly experimental cinematography. Any attempts to embrace the latter would have, more than likely, reduced these films' audience, whose numbers were already threatened, to the vanishing point by the attraction of decensored foreign commercial imports.

One of the sustained concerns of the analyses that follow is to assess the ideological consequences, first, of the appeal to parameters of meaning established by the overall climate of redemocratization and, second, the utilization of semiotic strategies to ensure the films function as texts that are not Hollywood competitors but entries in a new socially analytical Argentine filmography.

HISTORICAL CONTEXTS

■ ■ ■
Camila: Beauty and Bestiality

Overdetermination refers to a complex of features and strategies of texts that constitute emphasis added to its constituents. In line with the view that texts are organized in accord with coherent (although not always coherently applied) semiotic principles, the signs of a text recur at certain intervals in order to ensure that specific patterns of meaning are there to be discerned by the reader. The exact interpretation assigned to these patterns by the reader may diverge widely, and the patterns of convergence may even be discerned in different ways by different readers, but nearly all readers approach a text with the assumption that there is a meaning there to be experienced and that the text will engage in a number of discourse strategies in order to ensure that that meaning cannot be missed.

Overdetermination is an essential defining feature of conscientiously elaborated cultural texts, to the extent that the randomness associated with the lived social text (itself a natural cultural text through the mediating force of societal ideologies) is counterbalanced by the semiotic efficiency presumed to distinguish the former. To be sure, if meaning is not inherent in texts, natural or elaborated, but is rather the result of an applied reading—that is, of an elaborated secondary text—then the natural social text may be demonstrated to be overdetermined if the interpreter demonstrates convincingly that there is an unusually efficient confluence of signification in the random flow of events framed for analysis. A good example of reading an overdetermination in the social text is what Joan Didion has called the "mystification of rape," the proposition that somehow rape is different from other forms of violent

14

crime, particularly in its social meaning.[1] But even if this is so, the interpretive efforts of the secondary text are counterbalanced by an invested overdetermination, with which elaborated texts are alleged to have been invested by an authorial hand, whereas, the hand-of-God view of human history aside, natural social texts cannot reasonably be viewed to have been forged by authorial elaboration. At the same time, and as a densification of the processes of meaning involved, primary elaborated cultural texts may engage in charting overdeterminations in the social or historical text as part of their intertextuality with "real life," especially where documentalism and archival expropriation are involved. This is certainly true in the case of texts called historical in the conventional sense of making use of material drawn from a society's record of the accumulated past.

Overdetermination as a compositional practice for confirming a certain meaning effect and encouraging specific interpretations cannot, however, lead to closed texts, at least within the realm of what Western societies have considered to be sophisticated cultural production. Texts whose meaning is too easily derivable, too easily conducive to interpretational consensus, in addition to being viewed as boring, are, more important, taken to be manipulative; they "force" a meaning upon the reader via an overdetermination that is coercive because it forecloses any ambiguity, any doubt, any relativity. Trivial cultural texts like advertising, popular songs, greeting card verse, political speeches, religious sermons, most television programming, and the bulk of Hollywood movies are overdetermined in this fashion and are thus viewed, at least by cultural sophisticates, to be ideologically manipulative and therefore pacifying. Those same sophisticates, though, may attempt to open up popular culture texts by reinscribing them within a critical framework that reassigns their semiotic processes in such a way as to produce ironic, self-reflective, and contestatorial readings.[2]

Rather, overdetermination is balanced with strategies of ambiguity deployed in conjunction with the premise that meaning is, in any event, intrinsically ambiguous, which is why overdetermination is necessary in the first place. These strategies provide a text with an openness that allows the reader to be a coparticipant in

1. Susan Brownmiller, *Against Our Will: Men, Women, and Rape,* and Andrea Dworkin, *Intercourse.*
2. Andrew Ross, *No Respect: Intellectuals and Popular Culture.*

the act of semiosis rather than a passive (and pacified) recipient of totalized meanings. It is assumed that a critical analysis of the cultural text and, through it, of the historical reality it is rewriting, will flow from such forms of reader engagement. The production of meaning thus becomes work for the reader, with all of the beneficent resonances such socialized efforts entail in our society. Typically, overdetermination may be offset by structural asymmetries, various forms of troping established patterns, ellipsis, and a general distortion of expected narrative morphology—in short, any procedure that will counteract the closure deriving from the unquestioned conventionality induced by rigid overdetermination.

A film like María Luisa Bemberg's *Camila* (1984) is an interesting example of sustained narrative overdeterminations, and at the same time it introduces significant punctuative ruptures for the purpose of encouraging a revised reading of the evoked historical text, a reading that can be generally characterized as politically feminist.

Camila retells the story of Camila O'Gorman, the daughter of a wealthy Creole landowner during the dictatorship of Juan Manuel de Rosas in mid-nineteenth-century Argentina. O'Gorman senior supported Rosas's federalist policies. Rosas's power, based on a violence endorsed by populist sentiment, prefigured the institutionalization of human rights abuses, the systematic use of torture, the disappearance and liquidation of dissenters, and the appeal to state terrorism as a means for social control. The spectator must naturally assume a continuity between Rosas's bloody Restauración de las Leyes (Restoration of the Laws) and, almost one hundred and fifty years later, the military's *guerra sucia* (dirty war) and the Proceso de Reorganización Nacional. This sort of correlation is something like a zero degree of interpretation, in the sense of there being virtually no latitude for exception, in all those Argentine films that appeal to significant moments in the national historical record as part of an effort to provide an interpretation of recent Argentine society under military tyranny.

Camila O'Gorman led the highly protected and ordered life of a child of the early Argentine oligarchy, secure in the wealth of her father and the position it provided her in Porteño society. Yet, Camila deviated from the accepted path by falling in love with a priest, Ladislao Gutiérrez. The two fled to the northern frontier, she became pregnant, and they were discovered and brought back to Buenos Aires. They were executed on August 18, 1848, by a

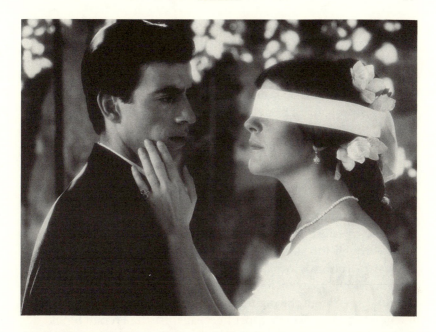

Susú Pecoraro as Camila O'Gorman discovers Imanol Arias as Father Ladislao Gutiérrez during a game of blindman's buff in *Camila,* and later faces death by firing squad. The contrast between the white and the black blindfolds signifies Camila's awakening to Eros and her death at the hands of the patriarchy.

firing squad in Santos Lugares, the site of Rosas's country estate outside Buenos Aires. Camila immediately entered Argentine folklore as a symbol both of Rosas's bloody persecution and of a feminine mystique of sacrifice at the hands of male brutishness.[3] Camila's and Ladislao's deaths, hardly a fitting punishment for what was probably a noncodified offense, involved the execution of the daughter of one of Rosas's staunch supporters, thereby confirming an image of tyrannical excesses amply exploited by the anti-Rosas resistance inside Argentina and abroad.

Bemberg's treatment of the Camila legend recruits multiple forms of narrative overdetermination. The film is dominated by the images of the Terror imposed during the Rosas regime (1829–1852). Rosas was able to consolidate his central power as governor of Buenos Aires through the skillful elimination of rival *caudillos* (political bosses) in the provinces, thereby imposing Buenos Aires as the *primus inter pares* in what was supposed to be a federation of provinces, through the manipulation of British interests (basically, the need for Argentine export beef) against the French blockade; and by the assassination or exile, chiefly to Chile or Uruguay, of opposition within his own Federales or of the Unitarios, who championed a strong central government based in Buenos Aires and tied to European commercial interests. Rosas was able to marshal populist sentiment against the aristocrats and merchants who had led the revolt against Spain—a populist sentiment resentful of the wealth and privilege that seemed to flow from their leadership and foreign alliances. Rosas's appeal was based on his self-identification as the Restaurador de las Leyes and his programmatic evocation of Hispanic and Creole cultural motifs: colloquial Argentine Spanish, primitive Catholicism, folkloristic practices, telluric symbols, and, most of all, loyalty to charismatic leaders—the *caudillo* tradition incarnate. The fact that these motifs were underlain by a violence deriving from the harsh realities of survival in an impoverished and remote colonial backwater allowed Rosas, with bloody implacability, to persecute opposition to his increasing authority (particularly during the late 1830s and early 1840s).

The Rosas opposition rhetoricized the practices of the Terror in order to generate international opinion against the Restaurador

3. John Lynch, *Argentine Dictator: Juan Manuel de Rosas, 1829–1852*, 239–41; and Manuel Vizoso Gorostiaga, *Camila O'Gorman y su época*.

and the policies of national destiny he stood for and to unite opposition from within.[4] But there is no reason to believe that the bloodletting of the Terror was any different in form or degree from the violent civil wars that had characterized the realignments of political power throughout Latin America in the decades following independence from Spain. Rosas encouraged the activities of a special vigilante group, the Mazorca, which became the archsymbol of the Terror. José Mármol in his novel calls them the Mashorca, stressing an etymology referring to the gallows, although their procedure was in fact to slit the victim's throat with a dull knife. Eduardo Gutiérrez, on the other hand, sticks to the preferred spelling and attributes the name, which means "corncob," to the use of this agricultural byproduct in a final indignity practiced on the corpses of the vigilantes' victims. Yet such groups of marauding supporters, manipulated by the *caudillo,* were an integral part of populist political power.

A film like *Camila* will evoke in the Argentine audience, in addition to the paradigmatic images of Rosas enshrined in the national historical consciousness, all the projections of Rosas alleged to exist in subsequent history. The forces that eventually toppled Rosas inspired the history books that have educated Argentines for over a century, beginning with the ones by Bartolomé Mitre, founder of the oligarchic newspaper *La Nación* and later president of the country. The figure of Rosas himself, who significantly does not appear in Bemberg's film, for many prefigures *caudillo*-style presidents like Hipólito Yrigoyen, but most especially Juan Domingo Perón. But in a pattern of correlations established between Rosas and all the military dictators except Perón, who, though he came from the military, was democratically elected, the lack of charisma-induced populist support for the generals has meant that what is emphasized are the dimensions of state terrorism.[5] Specifically, the agents of the *guerra sucia* and the *proceso* instituted after the March 1976 coup—thugs who had their paramilitary roots in the Asociación Anticomunista Argentina (Argentine Anticommunist Association)—are understood to be spiritual heirs of

4. Two significant examples are José Mármol's *Amalia* (1851–1855), contemporaneous with the Terror, and Eduardo Gutiérrez's *Juan Manuel de Rosas: los dramas del terror* (1882), part of the post-Rosas revisionism.

5. Fleur Cowles establishes this correlation in his *Bloody Precedent: The Perón Story.*

the Mazorca; and the unmarked black Ford Falcons in which they careened around Buenos Aires in their blackguardly operations had all of the horrifying symbolism of the Mazorca's red streamers and decorative corncobs.[6]

But more than merely suggesting the correspondences between Rosas and subsequent *caudillos* or between the Mazorca and secret police corps, a film like *Camila* overdetermines, both horizontally (the axis of Camila's personal story) and vertically (the axis of historical meaning), resonances concerning a climate of repressive terror. An ideology, supported multiply by the apparatus of state terror, circumscribes Camila's exercise of individual rights as recognized by the dominant intellectual movements of the nineteenth century. These rights are encoded in the spirit of romanticism in the form of individual self-expression, with the paradigmatic form of that expression being the practice of sentimental love. Camila's tragic flaw is the belief that she can pursue unhindered a relationship with the priest Ladislao, that the love between them ought to triumph over social conventions (Church and parental condemnations) and political considerations, or the shifting alliance between Rosas and Church hierarchy. Rosas is willing to execute the illicit lovers in order to affirm his commitment to Christian morality. Lulled by the naivete afforded by protection her father receives in his support for Rosas, Camila is insufficiently aware of how the personal is political. In Bemberg's film, Camila is the aggressive sexual partner, and she embarks on a course of action based on a fatal misreading of established sociopolitical codes.

Narrative overdetermination exists horizontally in the film in the form of multiple associations to be made between Camila's story and the experiences with repression of subsequent generations of Argentine citizens: a personal relationship that exceeds the bounds of a harshly enforced public morality; the activities of spies, secret agents, and informers who allow no protection in any corner of the private domain; the cynical exercise of power by individuals for whom individual rights have no meaning and are, indeed, a threat to the consolidation of power; a pattern of systematic betrayal that subverts allegiances forged by value systems now considered secondary to the operations of power consolidation;

6. Ford Falcons were chosen partly in remembrance of Police Chief Ramón Falcón, assassinated in 1909 by a Jew.

and, most significantly, the trivialization of the personal. The last may be viewed as a consequence of the enforcement of the institutional over the personal as a part of consolidation of power.

Specifically, Camila discovers that her destruction at the hands of the political process is epitomized by her father's willingness to sacrifice her. She had seen how he supported the Rosas regime and accepted without a murmur the public manifestations of the Terror; among others, the book dealer who supplied her and her intimates with banned reading falls victim to the Mazorca, and she sees his severed head on display on her way to church one morning. She had seen how her father was willing to imprison his mother forever, under orders from the government, in the attic of his house in punishment for her amorous extravagances that included an alleged French spy.[7] And she had seen how he was willing to force her to accept a convenient marriage as the normal lot of women. One of the most delicious sequences of the film involves an interview between Camila and her father over this matter. They are momentarily interrupted by a visit from, quite symbolically, Ladislao. When they resume their conversation, the father inquires what they were talking about. Camila's previously silent mother says, "Imprisonment." No, the father says, it was marriage. "It's the same thing," Sra. de O'Gorman retorts tartly, as she continues to rock and sew.

Yet none of these prefigurations prepares Camila for the way in which her father, to affirm his loyalty to Rosas and his own support for conventional morality, is able to acquiesce in his daughter's execution, even though that execution is in violation of a constitutional guarantee against the death penalty for pregnant women. Sr. O'Gorman is, thus, the real villain of the film, and not the absent Rosas. As a consequence, the implication is not that Rosas's power reaches out and contaminates the father's allegiance to Camila. Rather, it is that Rosas is the abstract synthesis of a form of patriarchal power manifested eloquently in this one case by O'Gorman's sacrifice of his daughter, and elsewhere by a constellation of indignities against a presumed spirit of individual liberties.

Camila is a feminist film in its semiotic investment in specify-

7. Sandra M. Gilbert and Susan Gubar's epygonic motif in their *Madwoman in the Attic* is evoked here—women who are considered mad, and are often driven to madness, for their refusal to abide by the conventions of female submissiveness. The correlation between the sexual and the political in Bemberg's film is briefly discussed by Rich, "An/Other View of New Latin American Cinema," 17.

ing patriarchal oppression from the bottom up. The power of the father is encoded out into successive circles of repression, to be returned to the personal in the way in which the most abstract symbols of the patriarchal ideology permeate a society downward as signs for a "proper" and "normal" human conduct. Camila's exercise of a personal choice in sentimental love is given contemporary feminist dimensions in her role as the assertive partner—a role epitomized by the fact that, in a key scene, it is Ladislao's derriere and not Camila's that is showcased in the obligatory but now wryly ironic gesture of sex-symbolization. Feminist dimensions are also evident in the ways in which she is the morally superior one when they are discovered, imprisoned, and executed. Ladislao whines like a whipped puppy, throws himself at the foot of the altar he believes he has offended, and sweats profusely as he is led to his execution. While torn by profound suffering, Camila is nevertheless the stronger of the two, and her words of love to Ladislao that echo as they are placed in their respective coffins close the film: "Ladislao, aquí estoy, mi amor" (Ladislao, my love, I am right here).

Camila is overdetermined horizontally in the accretion of evidence regarding her father's villainy. O'Gorman is masterfully, if in a somewhat typecast fashion, played by Héctor Alterio, who plays Norma Aleandro's corrupt husband in *The Official Story* in addition to numerous other dastardly roles in Argentine and Spanish films.[8] Besides the manifestations of patriarchal authority already mentioned, O'Gorman strides through the film giving orders, imposing silences, and engaging in activities that assert his control. The film opens with his reception of his mother as she arrives by coach for her immurement in his attic (actually the *mirador,* or widow's walk, of a colonial household). The interview between them is marked by his unctuous superiority—"Mama, I hope you will be very happy here"—and her dripping sarcasm in the face of the rituals of courtesy that cannot hide the fact that she is turning herself over to her prison warden in the person of her own son.

Bemberg's correlation between the symbols of patriarchal authority and the major points in Camila's story as a sacrificial victim

8. Alterio is also remembered as the fascist military officer killed by his own daughter in Carlos Saura's 1975 *Cría cuervos* (Raise crows); most recently he is Sor Juana Inés de la Cruz's leering ecclesiastical nemesis in Bemberg's 1990 *Yo, la peor de todas* (I, the worst of all).

comes close to being overdetermined to the point of interpretive closure. This is perhaps most dramatically underscored by the scene in which Camila's brother rushes to inform their father that she and Ladislao have been found. As a reminder to the viewer, that ranching is the mainstay of his and Argentina's wealth, O'Gorman is engaged in butchering some cattle and is covered with blood. In his anger over the news, he strikes his son and then dashes off to fulfill his paternal responsibilities to insure punishment for his wayward child. With the blood underscoring the enforcement of social codes via physical violence, and butchering recalling the practices of the Mazorca and the demand for sacrificial slaughter, this sequence prefigures the denouement of the last half hour of the film.

When the semiotic lines of force of *Camila* begin to emerge in a definitive fashion, it becomes clear that the film is structured around an interplay between Camila and her father, which is, again, why Rosas is no more than a remote presence and how what is involved can be viewed as fundamentally a feminist correlation between Camila's personal story and a dominant Argentine political tradition of repression through the instrumental institution of the patriarchy. Bemberg chooses to provide filmic plotting of this relationship in terms of the figures of the Beauty and the Beast. The Beauty is, of course, Camila, and the Beast is her father. In traditional versions of this motif, the young virgin is saved from rape (or its metaphors) by a masculine figure, either her father or various paternal stand-ins. In *Camila,* however, the woman is no longer a virgin; she is not being saved from her ravisher but rather torn from the lover she has chosen and seduced; and the separation is brought about by her father, a figure invested with multiple patriarchal meanings in his relationship with Camila, with his family as a unit, with his society (community, commerce, church), and with his government.

Camila is perhaps one of the most visually beautiful Argentine films of recent decades. Underwritten in part with money from Spanish sources and shot in and around the colonial museum at Chascomús in the province of Buenos Aires, the film has as one of its merits the meticulous reconstruction of the clothing and the decor of early nineteenth-century Argentina. And the Argentine actress Susú Pecoraro and the Spanish actor Imanol Arias are extremely attractive additions to the physical settings of the movie.

The person of Camila is an alluring combination of the feminine demureness associated with nineteenth-century upper-class womanhood and the assertive independence provided by her complete awareness of her privileged position in society. This sense of independence, appropriately enhanced by gestures of what the modern spectator would call a feminist consciousness (if only an unconscious one), is what puts the plot in motion. Camila demonstrates her independence in her reading, in her topics of conversations with the members of her circle, in her calm resistance to her father's more imperious demands, and, finally, in the way in which she sets out to win Ladislao sexually. The fact that Camila ignores—perhaps blindly, but the more interesting possibility is that it is an act of deliberate defiance—what the repercussions will be of her daring assertiveness provides the dramatic interest of her story. Her disregard is presumably to be read as an index of the innocence that exonerates her both in the Argentine popular tradition and for Bemberg's contemporary spectators. Thus, Camila is a Beauty in both body and soul, and her beauty derives in equal measures from her commitment to what she feels is her natural right to sexual fulfillment and the exemplary deliberateness with which she pursues Ladislao and handles his masculine limitations (first his timidity, then his vacillations, and then his cowardice). Camila stands alone. True, there is some measure of support from people around her, but the destiny she has charted for herself requires, in the universe of the film, that the plot turn on Camila versus the Others, a strategy that enhances the unambiguous, that is, overdetermined, meanings with which the woman is invested.

O'Gorman, by contrast and despite all of the attention-getting qualities of Alterio's brutish persona, is only an extension of the forces of repression that swirl around his daughter. Even Ladislao, whenever he falls short of Camila's intense commitment to their love—on one occasion she states, "I'm jealous of God,"—projects repression, most notably when he throws himself at the foot of the altar after the two fugitives have been denounced to Rosas's agents. In this sense, beastliness permeates the universe of *Camila,* and O'Gorman is only its most efficient, and vocal, spokesman. The Father is everywhere for Camila.

Camila's flight from her father's home and from Buenos Aires and her refuge with Ladislao in the Corrientes hinterland cannot be an effective escape, since she is still a part of human society and

even in Ladislao's arms she is cradled by an extension of the patriarchy. It is for this reason that there is no escape from the Beast
for Camila, no place where she can stand outside the shadow it
casts on her life, and her literal death at the end of the story is the
logical culmination of the various mortal effects of repression on
the victim. In the traditional tale, the Beauty is saved from Wicked
Beast, but this is only possible if the savior is an extension of an all-
powerful force of social order. When the aggressor is that social
order, escape from the clutches of the Beast becomes immensely
problematical.[9] And the elements of overdetermination in *Camila*
are indexes of those problems that are ultimately inescapable for
Camila and for whatever components of Argentine social history
she is read to personify.

Yet there is an incredible irony in Bemberg's film. *Camila* finds
it necessary to confirm the strength of its heroine's commitment to
love by closing the film with a long and melodramatic execution
sequence. We witness Camila's despair as she realizes that no one
can step forward to save her, her baby, and her lover from being
shot, and we witness the counterpoint between that despair and
the cynical declarations of the representatives of the regime as they
justify the execution. We witness the conduct of the execution,
including the refusal by several soldiers to fire on Camila. And we
witness the procedure of placing the bodies in their respective
caskets, with the voice-over of Camila's declaration of eternal presence for Ladislao. This soap-operatic denouement functions to
overdetermine the romantic motifs of love's strength in the face of
the full weight of social adversity, and it is every bit as emotion
drenched as any number of classic Hollywood tearjerkers.[10] The
high intensity of the last twenty minutes derails the film completely into the thicket of conventional narrativity. With all the
strands of meaning woven firmly together and overdetermined as
to the unequivocal emotional impact they are designed to produce, *Camila* reaffirms its heroine's commitment of Ladislao. To

9. Indeed, in the classic version of the tale, the Beauty ends up falling in love
with the Beast and discovering his inner beauty, which, in an ironic formulation,
would be tantamount to her becoming enamored of the very social order that
represses her.

10. Schumann, *Historia del cine latinoamericano,* 44.

be sure, the reaffirmation thoroughly departs from the historical record, since the closing voice-over is pure cinematographic fiction. One supposes this is meant to assert Camila's unswerving faith in her own choices while at the same time articulating her dominant role as a woman in the relationship with Ladislao.

At the same time that Camila reasserts her erotic and sentimental initiative, the film diverts attention from what would be an exception to the romantic overdetermination of Camila's character: the fact that her lover is himself a component of the patriarchal structures Camila had attempted to free herself from. Although the film is clear in its analysis of Ladislao's fear and reluctance in accepting Camila's sexual advances—and it is an analysis of a man's weaknesses that serves to confirm Camila's strengths as a woman—the viewer is left with the pastel-hued romantic image of Camila having chosen this man as her companion for all eternity. Thus the love story element in Bemberg's *Camila,* so insistent in the final segment of the film, is dramatically at odds with the themes of the rejection of social repression and the liberation of the individual through erotic fulfillment. Perhaps it would be unreasonable to expect a historical figure, and one circumscribed by legendary accounts, like Camila, to have any more effective option for her attempt at freedom from her father than Father Ladislao Gutiérrez. But the fact that Bemberg's film in the end loses sight of what Ladislao still continues to represent ("once a priest, always a priest") means that an unambiguously overdetermined and highly narrative love story must carry the final burden of meaning for the film.

▪ ▪ ▪

A Funny Dirty Little War (No habrá más penas ni olvido): Political Sectarianism as Farce

Of the many adjectives that could be marshalled to describe Peronism, one of the most nuclear must surely be "personalist," to the extent that the movement, the party, and its various governmental tenures on all levels, including four presidential tenures (two cut short by military overthrows), were built around the figure of Juan Domingo Perón (1895–1974). As a consequence of such personalism, political theory and praxis became constructed after the fact of influence and power, beginning with the need to forge an additional coherence, beyond populist commitments, out of the leader's scattered casual verbal statements, formal and informal speeches, and published documents.

One of the most famous of these texts is the twenty principles enunciated by Perón in a speech on October 17, 1950, commemorating the anniversary of his release from prison in 1945 because of the public protests of his supporters, putatively led by Eva Duarte (whom he immediately married after his release). The sixth of the principles articulated in "Sobre las verdades fundamentales del justicialismo" (On the fundamental truths of justicialism) asserts: "For a Peronist there can be nothing better than another Peronist." An often heard, snappier variant suppresses the modal verb: "For a Peronist there is nothing better than another Peronist." This sixth principle may not be the most crucial of the twenty, but around it turns a significant stage in the evolution of Peronism in Argentine politics: the disastrous internal dissensions in the movement in the early seventies, some of which survive into the present.

Certainly there is nothing unusual about a broad-based and populist political movement revealing major rifts for combined reasons of ideology and the usual jockeying for power of widely diverse components. But what happened to Peronism in the early seventies went beyond the customary internal divisions of expansive populism. Also, the Peronistas had only in part to do with the fact that the movement functioned in a personalist fashion around an individual whose pronouncements may have been as much contradictory because of age and infirmity as they were enigmatic because of political shrewdness. The fact is that, in order for Peronism to move toward vying for relegitimation (it had been banned for almost twenty years after Perón was deposed in 1955) and to compete successfully in the changed electoral scene of 1973, it was necessary for the movement to expand its ideological scope substantially and to include elements that, in many ways, were in frank contradiction with Peronism's original "national socialist" roots. Specifically, patriarchal hard-liners had little use for the Che Guevara–style revolutionary Marxists and trade union socialist reformers who were assimilated under the umbrella of Peronism in order to insure its electoral victory and to pave the way for Perón's return. Indeed, the official presidential candidate, Héctor Cámpora, was spokesman for the incorporation of the revolutionary left, and he was one of the first victims of the purges that began within party ranks when Perón did return to Argentina in June 1973 to undertake (or to see undertaken in his name) the redefinition of the party's power hierarchy and ideological discipline along restorative and reactionary (in the basic sense of the word) lines.

Between Cámpora's election in 1973 and the reimposition of military rule in March 1976 with the overthrow of Perón's vice-presidential successor María Martínez de Perón (Isabelita), Peronism set out to eliminate the whole left apparatus. In the process a number of miscellaneous political accounts were settled violently in other sectors of the party. Isabelita's administration made the process of left-wing extermination government policy, and it was continued by the military regimes in the form of the so-called *guerra sucia.* Consequently, Peronism may have been realigned along traditional lines, but both the party and the country were nearly destroyed. All of the complex machinations of the struggles for political power produced accusations, violent dissension, assassinations, arrests, torture, and executions. Thus, in writing the history of Peronism in the 1970s, and within the context of the *guerra sucia,* two of the most significant topics are the increasingly dangerous role for the left under the Peronista umbrella and its ultimate bloody elimination.

The Peronista principle transcribed above is, although originally contained in a speech, reproduced in *El libro rojo de Perón* (The red book of Perón, 158), a pocket-sized collection of apothegms attributed to Perón. This publication, dated April 1973 and published by A. Peña Lillo, a publishing house tied to left-wing Peronista interests, is a direct imitation of the then much popularized *Mao's Little Red Book.* This publication was part of the iconography of Perón as a left-wing ideal, an identification that was pursued perhaps more vigorously and successfully with reference to Eva Perón, as synthesized in the slogan "If Evita were alive, she'd be a *montonera.*" (The *montoneros* were one of the armed nationalist revolutionary groups, named after gaucho independence fighters of the nineteenth century.)

The statement "For a Peronist there is nothing better than another Peronist" figures prominently in Héctor Olivera's *No habrá más penas ni olvido* (1983), based on Osvaldo Soriano's 1980 novel of the same name (translated into English in 1986 as *A Funny Dirty Little War*). A plaque bearing Perón's assertion is just one of the many signs of Peronist culture that appear in Olivera's movie, which is a scathing indictment of the liquidation of left-wing Peronist elements by the old power guard within the party and its neofascist allies. Olivera is most known for the internationally acclaimed *Rebellious Patagonia* (1974), based on the army's brutal breaking of a workers' strike in Patagonia in the 1910s, an event to be understood, as it is in the 1959 novel by David Viñas, *Los dueños de la tierra* (The masters of the land), on which *Rebellious Patagonia* is based, as part of the climate of authoritarianism-fascism that runs as a constant throughout modern Argentine history.[11] Obviously, for Olivera, whether or not Peronism is a component of authoritarian-fascist culture, the purge of the party's left-wing elements is of a whole with the tradition of *gorilismo* (right-wing thuggery), and the signs of such a belief are so transparent in *A Funny Dirty Little War* as to require virtually no comment.

Set in 1974 in Colonia Vela, an insignificant town in La Pampa province, Olivera's movie deals with the higher order to purge the municipal delegate for being an *infiltrado* (infiltrator), that is, a communist sympathizer who has infiltrated the party. (It is immaterial whether the order comes from the party or from the government, since they are now one and the same.) Fuentes is viewed as suspect primarily because his assistant is a known socialist and because his office is a hangout for young adults of known "Bolshevik" leanings who are anxious to have a say in the revolutionary affirmation of a "free" Argentina—free of foreign intervention and the machinations of military tyranny. It is to Olivera's credit that he does not spend any time ridiculing the youthful left, whose ideology was often little more coherent than that of the ruling party. Indeed, by 1983 it was not difficult to agree with Pablo Giussani's assessment of the middle-class revolutionary left, having adopted the style of Che Guevara, as "armed arrogance."[12] At the same time, Olivera does not find it necessary to romanticize them either, since the focus of the film is on the dynamics of the purge mentality as such.

What begins as the simple demand that the municipal delegate resign and take with him his "communist" followers escalates into

11. Viñas is one of Argentina's classic Marxist intellectuals.
12. Pablo Giussani, *Montoneros, la soberbia armada*.

a full-scale armed confrontation between, first, the delegate and the town police and then the mayor and his leather-jacketed thugs in dark eyeglasses, with the constant threat of the national army intervening. In the process, the delegate is taken prisoner, beaten up, tortured, and killed; a considerable amount of personal and public property is destroyed (including the town delegation, which is fired upon, bombed, rushed by a phalanx of tractors, and then burned to the ground); and various bystanders are insulted, assaulted, maimed, and killed. The distinctions may be difficult for the spectator having no extensive familiarity with the historical setting among loyal Peronistas whose allegiances go back to the founding days of the movement: rank-and-file good Peronist simple folk, called *los muchachos;* left-wing allies who sincerely feel they are contributing to the redefinition of Peronism as a socialist option; opportunists who seek to derive profit from an advantageous association; and paid thugs and assassins who do not care what the ideology of their bosses is. However, Olivera leaves no room for doubt that the point of his film turns on the politics of liquidation and the free-ranging violence that flows from it.

Olivera's film, like Soriano's novel, is not conceived as documentary or docudrama, as faithful as it may be to basic facts about the purge of the *infiltrados* that foreshadowed the *guerra sucia.* Nor is it a symbol-charged allegory of key sociohistorical events, in the fashion of *Camila* or *The Official Story.* Rather, the modality of *A Funny Dirty Little War* is something like a black humor farce. Although farce may be considered an elemental force in all dramatic narrative comedy, as a traditional Western cultural genre it has been customarily applied to those works in which the emphasis is less on the development of character or on a comic or humorously ironic interpretation of human character, either generalized or individualized, and more on the broad, buffoonish, slapstick, even grotesque, consideration of dramatic acts in themselves. These acts may turn on situations that provoke them, on the substance of those acts (gestures, discourse styles, physical appearance), or on the specific behavior patterns or so-called life-styles that those acts generate. Farce, if it is to have any specific meaning, must be either transpersonal, in the sense of going beyond individuals or individual psychology, or interpersonal, in the sense of focusing on a particular level of deportment in human commerce.

A Funny Dirty Little War is farce to the extent that Olivera constructs a filmic narrative that outlines the grotesque, utterly insane consequences, in terms of human actions (beginning with verbal assault and ending in torture and execution), deriving from a particularly pathetic understanding of the dynamics of party politics. The internal workings of the Peronista party—workings that, because it is the party in power and virtually *the* state party, mean also the internal workings of the Argentine civil government—are portrayed as a combination of cynicism and utter stupidity. The cynicism is invested most eloquently in the person of Dr. Guglielmini, the local *intendente* (mayor) and Peronista authority, and the stupidity in the person of Suprino, Colonia Vela's Peronista political hack. Olivera's treatment of party politics moves between the silly, especially in the form of meaningless slogans (both the traditional Peronista ones and those coined to refer specifically to the question of the alleged left-wing *infiltrados*), and the grimly pathetic: the growing carnage from one blunder by the authorities after another.

The film's reinvestment of Peronista iconography with meaning—the visual symbols, the verbal tags, the avowed formulas, the painted slogans—unquestionably points toward the ridicule, if not of Perón and Peronism in an overall sense, at least of what the movement had become as a political party by the early 1970s and as the political party exercising power from the capital of Buenos Aires down to sleepy hamlets like Colonia Vela. Olivera's prima facie ridiculing of Peronism at the time of the 1983 presidential elections (it opened on September 22, only weeks before voting took place) was a gamble that the Peronistas would not win the elections, and they did not, in an important electoral repudiation of precisely the history *A Funny Dirty Little War* represents.

Yet, it is not enough for *A Funny Dirty Little War* only to address the internal power struggles of Peronism. Olivera's film involves multiple sectors of society, including government leaders; bureaucrats; the police; private citizens of different social classes, occupations, and age groups; and even two well-dressed matrons who, like a dithering Greek chorus, appear strategically to utter surprised platitudes (of the "Dios mío" variety) in the best Argentine know-nothing tradition. Thus it is entirely plausible to project its semantic range beyond that of a caricature of Peronism and to see it functioning as a conceit on how Peronism is a vast synecdoche of the Argentine political process in both its synchronic and diachronic dimensions. The ideas that government exists to serve the self-interest of those occupying the slots of power structure and that party, government, and society together constitute a personalist projection of one's visionary grandeur and base meanness are firmly embodied in one understanding of how politics work in Argentina—or Latin America or anywhere in the world.

One ideological practice during redemocratization was to use films and cultural documents to establish homologies between contemporary structures of repression and tyrannical practices that reach back, even beyond the events surrounding Camila's persecution, to the earliest days of the nation. María Luisa Bemberg's film *Camila* and Ricardo Piglia's novel *Respiración artificial* (1988) exemplify the practice; but, then, this is something Ernesto Sabato had already done in *Sobre héroes y tumbas* (On heroes and tombs) in 1962. The allegorical mode of political interpretation may be found in now classic novels like Julio Cortázar's *Los premios* (The winners), published in 1960; Leopoldo Marechal's *El banquete de Severo Arcángel* (The banquet of Severo Archangel), published in 1965; and Marco Denevi's *Ceremonia secreta* (Secret ceremony), published in 1968. Many texts dealing with the projection of personalist politics and the clash between social idealism and the machinations of such politics could be cited, but one need go no further than Viñas's *Los dueños de la tierra* (The masters of the land), the novel on which Olivera's *Rebellious Patagonia* is based, wherein narrative events are dominated by the specter of the ward boss become president, Hipólito Yrigoyen.[13] He was deposed by Argentina's first military coup, which was of fascist inspiration and was, for many, a prefiguration of Juan Domingo Perón.

Thus, the proposition that *A Funny Dirty Little War* is basically a narrative treatment of the pathos of the Argentine political process explains the totalizing dimensions of its social panorama, both the way in which multiple facets of the populace are represented and the way in which all are implacably drawn into events, with the inevitability of high tragedy but without a tragic anagnorisis anchored in any individual consciousness—again, one reason for calling the film a farce. Olivera builds the narrative scheme

13. Yrigoyen was president from 1916 through 1922 and from 1928 through 1930.

by incorporating growing numbers of individuals and the societal sectors they represent, until, by the end of the film, the metaphor of trivial events having snowballed, he demonstrates how all members of the Colonia Vela microcosm are profoundly affected by what was initially a matter of a political party's internal power jockeyings. Such jockeyings may be truly momentous in party headquarters in Buenos Aires, but they are pettily absurd at the hamlet level. The focal point of the accusation of infiltration, the town clerk Mateo, is so pathetic in his meekness and so venal in his betrayal of the municipal delegate who has protected him that any narrative based on him would be inconceivable.

Rather, Mateo is as much a pretext for the puffery of the local political hack Suprino as he is for the film's narrative of a national political process beyond local politics and beyond Peronism itself. *A Funny Dirty Little War* is a veritable anthology of the clichés of self-serving politics in every quarter, and it is again a feature of the film as farce that no individual serves as a focal point for a moral investment against political posturing, as a bracketed individual driven by complex psychological motives. The figure of the municipal delegate, Fuentes, is played by Federico Luppi in yet another reincarnation of the staunch Argentine John Wayne type he has portrayed in seemingly countless films over the last three decades. Although here he is a paradigm of the *desaparecido* (disappeared person) in the sense that his body is the locus of persecution, torture, and illegal execution, he is never driven by anything other than firm-jawed self-pride. As an official elected by the people, he will not resign, and he is just as willing to set in motion expanding waves of violence, in the form of embattled resistance, as are those who are out to depose him, with the result that everything falls in the wake of the confrontation between the two forces.

The closest thing to an anchor point of personal redemption that transcends the scope of petty politics translated into massacre is the crop duster Cerviño, played masterfully by Ulises Dumont, one of Argentina's greater character actors. He literally transcends the political fracas, but not in the end the massacre, in his piper cub, El Torito. Cerviño, a stereotype of the Peronista *buen pibe* (good guy), is somewhat demented, and when he sets out to assist Fuentes in the name of Peronista solidarity, he is abetted by Juan, the town drunk, who is both a regular guest in the jail and its

Federico Luppi and Rodolfo Ranni, representatives, respectively, of the
Peronist left and right, frame one of Perón's classic presidential images,
from *A Funny Dirty Little War.*

janitor. Both men are *locos divinos* (divinely inspired madmen),
and they anticipate the key figure of the madman around whom
Fernando Solanas's *Sur* (South Side) is organized.[14] As such, both
men signal a position outside the political process, but both also
function as signs of the pitiful examples of bedrock Peronista true
believers who are left behind by the confrontation between right-
wing bosses and left-wing juventud Peronista. Mention might also
be made here of a third *buen pibe,* the policeman García, who, as
he is manipulated by Fuentes in order to save Fuentes's skin, keeps

14. I believe that in Argentina divinely inspired madness is usually reserved for
women.

repeating "If only the general (Perón) could see me now!" In addition to being delightful as a good-natured eccentric who tells the thugs to "fuck off" (and is, of course, executed for it), Cerviño is the focal point of the nature of *A Funny Dirty Little War*'s farce. This emerges in his two attempts to divert the assault by the Peronista operatives on Fuentes and his supporters. The first involves his flying over the combat zone and dusting everyone thickly with DDT. Literally, Fuentes's persecutors are blinded, and the spectator may choose to read Cerviño's gesture as a sign of the clouds of obfuscation being produced by the government party's internal conflicts. Cerviño's second gesture is to replace the DDT in his tanks with pig manure in a statement about the Peronista leaders and their thugs that requires no further elaboration.

Unfortunately, Cerviño's two sorties, as much as they add to Olivera's characterization of the motives of Fuentes's enemies, are purely gratuitous acts, overdetermined by the paternalistic structure. The persecutors have no compunction in seeking the pilot out and, after he has evoked Perón in the name of an honest Peronism, murdering him. The obvious contribution Cerviño and Juan make to *A Funny Dirty Little·War* is in the confirmation of the elements of grotesque farce: the absolute disjunction between the alleged and the real importance of the political stakes at issue, the destruction and carnage that flow from them, and, in terms of the film's framing of them, the senselessness of the whole situation. Since the rhetorical highlighting Cerviño and Juan provide is abundantly clear, any interpretational importance assigned to them must lie in another dimension. Such a dimension is twofold. From one point of view, the two town lunatics establish, because of their eccentricities and their refusal to conjugate reality in the same way as the opposing political factions, a point of reference outside the structure of the events being portrayed. Whether or not spectators can identify in Juan or Cerviño any attitude of repudiation of the political system Olivera rewrites in terms of a struggle to the death between right- and left-wing factions, depends on a rather dubious assessment of common sense the two possess beyond their fellow townspeople. By maintaining the texture of his film within the confines of farce, it is questionable whether audiences wishing to substitute critical analytical serious-mindedness for farce can find a sufficient point of

A scene of the exaggerated police operation against presumed
communist infiltrators in *A Funny Dirty Little War*. Note the contrast
between the traditional buildings of the background and the modern
military equipment of the forces of repression.

reference in Juan and Cerviño, who seem principally to animate
themselves with cheap wine.

The second importance of Juan and Cerviño lies in the way in
which they are able to underscore perhaps the most terrible aspect
of the political realities featured in Olivera's farce: the absolute
inevitability of the working out of the events set in motion by the
authoritarian order from above to get rid of the Marxists. There
can be no surprises in the working out of the "story morphology"
of Olivera's film. The end is a foregone conclusion on both the
level of the film's plot and—since this is what is significant about *A
Funny Dirty Little War*—on the level of the events of history it

refers to. That is, once Fuentes decides to arm himself and to defend the municipal offices against the Peronista operatives, it can only be a question of the degree of violence that will take place, not whether violence will ensue. Viewing a film released in 1983 on events that took place in 1974, given the Argentine sociopolitical history that ensued during that ten-year gap as the direct result of what happened within Peronism in the 1970s, any spectator with only a minimal knowledge of recent Argentine history cannot be greatly surprised by the dimensions of the massacre, torture, and execution that occur. Any cultural document that possesses such a retrovisionary historical structure invites the reader to engage in a reassessment of the events described and the circumstances that provoked them. In the case of *A Funny Dirty Little War,* however, the framework of the farce provides the greatest amount of ideological interest because of the specific attitude it encourages the spectator to adopt toward the phenomenon of Peronism and the larger Argentine political process it evokes.

One of the recurring motifs of the film is the attempt by several individuals to downplay the mounting tensions and the first manifestations of violence. Through the repetition of commonplaces like "Nothing ever happens in this country, nothing" and "What country do you really think we're in?" the attempt is made to ignore the unavoidable. The result is that *A Funny Dirty Little War* is based on a social vision underwritten by denial, by the selective understanding of the political process, and by an exercise of the resources of power, both rhetorical and material. Social life then becomes lived as grotesque farce in which those in charge do not hesitate to set in motion the destruction of the town in order to "save" it from their ideological opponents. As the local political hack confesses ingenuously, "It got away from me." But if the spectator is asked to repudiate the grotesque farce of Argentine life as it is experienced in Colonia Vela, there is a very real question as to where political allegiance can lie outside the process described by the film. Juan and Cerviño have a certain charm as lunatics who briefly transcend in a minimal way the machinations of political power, but there is no investment in their farcical dimensions that permits the audience to envision a way out of the mess—a way, that is, to halt the implacable working out of the narrative plot.

Historical necessity, both as past events (what happened in 1974) and as present reality (the extent to which those events bespeak an ongoing Argentine political process), casts an impenetrable shadow over *A Funny Dirty Little War,* like the clouds of DDT and the dark rain of pig manure Cerviño dumps from his plane, and the question is where the spectator is to turn for any viable alternative. It is in this context that the tango motif of the title, a verse from Carlos Gardel's tango "Mi Buenos Aires querido," one of the great mythifying texts of Argentine culture, and the closing Peronista cliché, "It's a beautiful day, a Peronist day," could not be more bleakly ironic. When the question of the need to get rid of the *infiltrados* first arises as an order that must be obeyed without question, it is explained as part of the need to "normalize" things. As Olivera's film demonstrates, to normalize means both to impose an authoritarian norm and to confirm as natural a political process of dreadful violence. But it also means to normalize for the spectator a type of cultural document in which farce, because of its texture and the internal homologies it requires for its effect (that is, everyone and everything reinforcing each other as overdetermined signs of the same quality of the human condition), forecloses most efficiently any transcendent, corrective point of reference and accounts for how Cerviño's grounding and execution is of a whole with the semiotic economy of the film.

▪ ▪ ▪
The Official Story (La historia oficial): Truth and Consequences

There are three moments of moral anagnorisis for the principal character, Alicia, played by Norma Aleandro, in Luis Puenzo's *The Official Story* (film script by Aída Bortnik and Puenzo) and, by extension, for the spectator. All three moments are especially problematical for the foreign spectator, who is more likely than not to have a limited knowledge of recent Argentine sociopolitical history. This is of exceptional interest, given the recognition accorded the film outside Argentina, signaled particularly by the Oscar it received as the best foreign film of 1986.

The first moment comes approximately a third of the way into the movie. Ana, played by Chunchuna Villafañe, has returned to Argentina after a half-dozen years in exile. The time of the film is March 1983. The Falklands conflict has ended in humiliation for Argentina, most of all for the military, and despite efforts to retain some of its dignity and to shore up the fascist ideology that the military sustained during its seven years of brutal rule, it is a foregone conclusion that the country will return to institutional democracy. As part of the transition, nationals like Ana have begun to return; they are individuals who had gone into exile during the period of the *guerra sucia,* which was devoted to the extermination by any means of alleged left-wing subversives. (The adjective *alleged* is properly employed here, since no one was ever brought to trial for subversion under the legal code of the country during the years 1976 to 1983.) Ana and Alicia had been close schoolmates, and after a dinner one evening at Alicia's house, the two women, in a glow of sisterly camaraderie, begin again to share intimacies. Alicia inquires as to why Ana left Argentina so abruptly, and the latter takes a deep breath and unburdens herself of the story of her detention, incarceration, torture, and rape, and of then being dumped on the street after her captors determined that she really did not have any idea of the whereabouts of her former lover, an alleged terrorist. Alicia, full of sympathy, asks Ana why she never reported her abuse to the authorities. Incredulous at the naivete of Alicia's question, Ana asks with terrible irony: "And you, for example, how would you have made . . . the complaint, I mean. . . . To whom would you have presented the complaint!"[15]

The second moment of moral anagnorisis comes approximately two-thirds into the picture. Alicia has now had her consciousness rather thoroughly raised concerning the *guerra sucia* and has pretty much accepted the fact that her adopted daughter, Gaby, is one of the children born in captivity to mothers kept alive only long enough to give birth before being slaughtered. Her husband,

15. Aída Bortnik and Luis Puenzo, *La historia oficial,* 48. Hereafter cited parenthetically in the text by page number. Bortnik also collaborated with Puenzo on the script for the latter's 1989 film, *The Old Gringo,* his version of Carlos Fuentes's novel *Gringo viejo,* about Ambrose Bierce and the Mexican revolution, starring Jane Fonda and Gregory Peck. Bortnik enjoys considerable prestige as a dramatist. Her play *Papá querido* (Father dearest) was part of the 1982 cycle of Teatro Abierto, the theater movement that made cultural history with its defiance of censorship by the military government.

who has extensive business dealings with the military, brought the child home one day somewhat as one brings home a doll won at a fair. These children serve a double purpose. On the one hand, the babies are rewards parceled out to supporters of the regime. On the other hand, the "rescue" of these children is seen as part of a moral imperative to provide them a "proper moral upbringing" in a Catholic home free of the contamination of the subversive underworld of their parents. In the film, this program is affirmed specifically both by the churchgoing habits of Gaby's adoptive parents and by the assertions of the priest whom Alicia consults when she begins to have doubts about how Gaby came into her life.

In the pursuit of the truth about Gaby's origins, Alicia comes into contact with Sara, played by Chela Ruiz. The contact is established through an organization to aid the parents and grandparents of missing children in locating the babies who disappeared into the hands of the military's supporters. Alicia and Sara go one day to a café-bar, where Sara, who has seen Gaby from a distance, shows Alicia some treasured photographs of her daughter as a child, in which the resemblance to Gaby cannot be missed. Alicia, overcome with the realization that Sara must be her child's grandmother, begins to weep. Sara, with all of the firmness of a lower-middle-class woman who has received from life harsh blows that the comfortably situated Alicia cannot even imagine, looks at her sternly and says, with the wisdom born of having wept and discovered that it is of little use: "You mustn't cry. Crying doesn't help at all. . . . I know what I'm saying, crying doesn't help" (121).

The final moment of moral agnorisis comes at the end of the film. Alicia has sent her daughter to her in-laws' house in order to confront her husband alone. Roberto, played by Héctor Alterio, is in the process of attempting to extricate himself from the collapsing edifice of shady dealings with the military, fearing that he will suffer the same fate as several of his associates, who have been arrested by a civil legal apparatus now able to reassert institutional controls. It is equally apparent that nonmilitary associates of the regime have been sacrificed by the generals in an attempt to turn accusations of massive corruption and fraud away from themselves, in the name of the purity of the military institutions. As he hysterically deals with anonymous telephone calls, Roberto asks his wife where Gaby is. Alicia, now echoing the rhetoric of the

Madres de Plaza de Mayo, says, "It's terrible not to know where your daughter is" (132). At this point, Roberto, in a display of the macho brutality claimed to underlie the violence of the military regime, begins to rough Alicia up. In an act that is synecdochical of the forms of torture applied to the regime's victims, Roberto traps his wife's fingers in a doorjamb, producing a scream of pain that is deftly calculated to reverberate throughout the body of the spectator.

It is only a few minutes before Alicia leaves, slamming the door in Norah-like fashion, leaving the keys (always kept on the inside of the door in Latin America for security purposes) swinging eloquently in the center of the screen. But before Alicia makes her dramatic exit, she turns and embraces her husband. The meaning of this embrace is not immediately clear, although the spectator could well interpret it as a gesture of commiseration, perhaps in recognition of the suffering that still awaits them. This embrace is not in the published film script, which only says: "ALICIA looks sadly at ROBERTO. She almost touches his arm as a final gesture, while she goes toward the door of the apartment and leaves without turning around" (134). I do not know why the minimal gesture called for by the script has become an embrace in the film, but in either case the final sign of affection made by Alicia toward Roberto has intense moral significance as one of the three moments of anagnorisis for Alicia and the spectator who accompanies her in her quest for the truth.

Alicia is an upper-middle-class history teacher. *The Official Story* is nothing if not cleverly and often heavy-handedly ironic in its employment of cultural signs. Despite her professional life as a history teacher, Alicia is woefully ignorant about what is going on around her. We see her in many scenes with her teenage students, who in her eyes willfully and erroneously attempt to establish contacts between the early nineteenth-century period she is teaching them about and current events. Her colleague, a literature teacher named Benítez, played by the Chilean Patricio Contreras, is attracted to her and attempts to make her cognizant of what is happening in Argentina and why things have started to fall apart. Alicia is no fool and is a decent person; for instance, she decries the stupid cruelty displayed by their hostess, the wife of a general, at a dinner party at the beginning of the film. But she leads an isolated life in the elegant Belgrano Beverly Hills–like house her husband's business activities provide for her. Her daughter attends a stylish day school, she moves in the best commercial and cultural spaces Buenos Aires has to offer—spaces that were refurbished by the economy of the military dictatorship to serve the tastes of the high bourgeoisie that supported it—and she teaches in a school attended by young men whose background is similar to hers, although their youth makes many of them opponents of the military their parents presumably support. Therefore, Alicia's trajectory of discovery throughout *The Official Story* is a remedial process, as she acquires the sociopolitical information necessary to place herself and her role as Gaby's mother in the real-life context of contemporary Argentine history that life in her milieu has up until this point denied her or allowed her to deny herself. Alicia has lived the "official story" history of the military's Proceso de Reorganización Nacional, and it is that text which she is obliged to rewrite in a personal process of anagnorisis.

On the immediate level of explicit content, the phenomenal success—perhaps more international than Argentine—of *The Official Story* is easy to explain, even if one sets aside the stimulus provided by the hype over a technically very competent first film produced by someone whose prior professional experience had been in advertising, and with a script by a relatively unknown playwright. Puenzo's film deals in a straightforward fashion with the issue of military dictatorship in Argentina, a country close to American and European consciousness, and it does so by focusing on one of the most discussed aspects of the regime's oppressions—one about which there can be no moral ambiguities, no dilemma of conflicting ideologies. There are those who, seeking any means to undermine the Madres de Plaza de Mayo, lay the blame for "subversive" beliefs at the feet of irresponsible mothers who were not careful enough to provide their children with respect for national institutions, beginning, of course, with the military. But few could object to the clamor raised on behalf of disappeared children, no matter whether their mothers could be viewed as irresponsible or not. Indeed, one of the most efficient ways to discredit the Proceso and its *guerra sucia* has not been to question the Proceso's validity within the context of Argentine institutional crises nor to object to the *guerra sucia*'s violation of constitutional guarantees, but to appeal to the universal abhorrence of the clandestine dis-

tribution of innocent babes as booty to supporters of the dictatorship. The allegation that these children were being provided Christian homes did little to mitigate the outrage over the way in which
the newborns were severed from their mothers and placed with
new families. The placing of these children with non-blood-re-
lated adoptive parents effectively overrode the claims of family
ties by the children's relatives who themselves were not accused of
having been involved in subversion. While it is reasonable to assume that there are those who have been unconcerned about the
disappeared children, there has been enough international concern for their status, and for the problems of identifying them and
restoring them as best as possible to their biological families, to
ensure a clear sympathetic identity of the major social issue dealt
with in *The Official Story*. Whereas the film may focus on the
evolution of Alicia's consciousness, the reason that that evolution is
of greater importance for purposes of audience identification is
that it turns on her quest for information about Gaby's origins and
on her relationship with her husband because of those origins.

To the extent that the film depends on the spontaneous reaction
of an audience outraged over the plight of Gaby and sympathetic
with Alicia's growing sense of horror at the truth concerning that
plight, Puenzo is able to organize the rhetoric of *The Official Story*
so as to provide a fairly univocal condemnation of the period of
military dictatorship between 1976 and 1983. That condemnation
is based on an underscoring of the fraud, corruption, and massive
violations of human rights that enabled the military to affirm and
maintain its power, a metonym of which was the phenomenon of
the disappeared children. Through that metonym we recover a comprehensive image of the persecution of several tens of thousands of
individuals who suffered at the hands of the military apparatus for
various forms of alleged and in many cases nonexistent resistance
to the dictatorship. Although there is substantial international concern over the widespread violation of human rights during regimes
like that of the Proceso, including the denunciation of secret arrests, incarcerations, torture, executions, confiscation of household
property for personal use, and sundry derived outrages, it is more
than anything else the metonymic significance of the disappeared
children that most effectively defines the ideological lines drawn
by Puenzo's film.

In order to bring out these lines, Alicia must remain essentially unconscious of the sociohistorical process unfolding in the world around her, something rather difficult to believe, given the fact that the woman is a history teacher and moves in privileged cultural circles. But it is not so much that Alicia lacks essential information about the military government, the Proceso, and the goals of the *guerra sucia;* rather, she lacks the horizons necessary to process that information in ways summoned by the events described in the film. In a very real sense, Alicia signifies the sort of mentality that allows dictatorial power to be exercised. A certain amount of acquiescence by the overall populace is required, or, if not outright acceptance, at least not noticeable organized protest of issues that challenge unconstitutional administrations. The higher the individuals' location on the socioeconomic scale, the greater the importance of their willingness to endorse, if only passively, military regimes. Thus, while Roberto may be assumed to have enthusiastically welcomed the generals because of the commercial opportunities their government provides him with, and to have justified that enthusiasm by what ideological principles are at his disposal, Alicia is more of a bystander in that she has no significant reason not to go along with her husband's enthusiasm. Moments of doubt might exist, but they do not coalesce in any coherent way that would place her outside the society in which she so comfortably moves. We see that society portrayed during the opening half-hour of the film: the school where she teaches, her home, a dinner party, her daughter's expensive birthday celebration—all of which is preceded by the resonant Argentine national anthem opening both the film and the academic year. Well-dressed and self-confident, Alicia sweeps through these spaces with all the bearing of a woman totally in command of her life. She represents exactly the sort of domestic security counted on by the regime as part of the process of maintaining legitimacy. As long as someone like Alicia is satisfied with her world, there can, short of a massive popular uprising, be no serious threat to the dictatorship. And even if an uprising were to occur, continued support by the privileged middle class would provide legitimation for squelching popular demands. Thus Alicia's lack of interpretive horizons is, no matter how real or natural, necessary to the structure of the film, since it is through her discovery of truth that this cultural document expounds to the spectator on the consequences of authoritarian military rule.

If it is possible to argue that military authoritarianism can constitute a legitimate form of republican government, constitutional or otherwise, such an issue does not enter into the universe of meaning of Puenzo's film. The same may be said for an even more crucial question concerning the ambiguity of right and wrong and of the commitment of individuals to positions of support and opposition for such governments. It is consistent with real-world sociopolitics to insist that a sufficient number of Argentines moved back and forth between support and repudiation of the Proceso, with enough supporting it at any one time for it to stay in power between 1976 and 1983 and with enough support being lost after the Falklands conflict to make it seem sensible to the generals to return the country to institutional democracy and to retreat with some semblance of dignity to their garrisons. None of this ambiguity, however, is transmitted by *The Official Story,* not even with reference to Alicia, who demonstrates, rather than ambivalence, movement toward an active personal position, which happens to be in opposition to the authoritarian regime as personified by her husband. Significantly, it is he whom she repudiates as the one most directly responsible for the acquisition of Gaby and the moral dilemmas that have flowed from that fact. Only indirectly is the authoritarian regime on which his power is based repudiated.

Textual verisimilitude is a criterion of paramount importance in a cultural document directed toward a mass, nonexperimental audience with a set of expectations concerning the nucleus of sociohistorical realism necessarily present in a film laying claims to the representation of real-world truths. In terms of such truths, the result of Alicia's indirect repudiation of the authoritarian regime is that Roberto's manipulation of the possibilities of authoritarian and dictatorial powers is matched by her willingness to trade knowledge for naivete. When that trade-off is no longer possible, when she is driven by a combination of factors—her students' restlessness, Benítez's barbs, Ana's political consciousness and quasi-feminist solidarity, the proddings of the organization committed to locating disappeared children, and Sara's personal quest— Alicia's inquisitiveness begins to overlap significantly with Roberto's cynicism to such a degree that her discovery of his complicity and the break between them becomes inevitable. It is only when Roberto's knowledge of how the system works is matched virtually point-by-point by Alicia's personal trajectory of discovery that the final scene is possible.

At the end of the film, the embrace that Alicia accords Roberto, even after he has slapped her around and crushed her fingers in the doorjamb, is in part a final gesture of matrimonial union between them, a sort of *omertà* by which Alicia signals her final discovery in all its plenitude of her husband's moral betrayal. The juxtaposition of this embrace with her abandonment of the patriarchal abode attests in only a few minutes to the before and after of their human relationship, the transition from wifely allegiance to resigned self-severance from the world that has both protected her and held her in thrall to an ignorance of sociopolitical realities. Yet Alicia's embrace may also be viewed as an almost parenthetical gesture toward a recognition of the ambiguities of human motivation and conduct that has up to this point been absent from the film. Whereas *The Official Story* has proceeded to mount a disjunctive categorization of the supporters of the military dictatorship, including Roberto and his business associates, and those opposed to it, including Ana, Benítez, some of Alicia's students, her father-in-law, the Madres de Plaza de Mayo, and other protestors—clearly the majority of the actors, in both senses of the word, in the film. Alicia's passive identification with the former and her defiant, assertive affiliation with the latter is, as a consequence, the basic narrative action of Puenzo's text. Thus, it is only at this final moment when Alicia knows she must separate from Roberto that the film reaches toward a second-level understanding of Roberto's situation. He is caught up in a corrupt system that is now in the process of betraying him in order to save the highest level of manipulators, the generals themselves. Roberto is the tragic figure of the film, because he has sold his soul and, in the process, created a horrible nightmare for Alicia and, by extension, for Gaby, who must at some point beyond the narrative sequence of *The Official Story* face the unknowns of her origin and, therefore, her lack of an institutionally defined place in society.

It is in Alicia's movement toward this final scene that she must confront, and ponder, the meaning of the other two moments of moral anagnorisis that I have identified in the film: her realization, first, that an aggrieved citizen has absolutely nowhere to turn for relief from systemic abuse in a society in which constitutional guarantees and institutional safeguards have been preempted by an authoritarian dictatorship, and, second, that in a society in which the individual has been reared to understand that such relief is nonexistent, it may not even be possible to contemplate the notion of relief. Yet, Argentines have historically been raised to believe that such relief is possible, even when that belief is mitigated by sardonic views concerning legendary inequities. A military regime that suspends the constitution "in order to protect it" creates a contradiction that makes possible the coherence of the absurd exchange between Alicia and Ana, underlain by the latter's pathetic irony in the face of her friend's naivete. It is within this context that the title of the testimonial by the current vice-president of Argentina, Eduardo Duhalde, *El estado terrorista* (The terrorist state) is no longer an oxymoron but a fully descriptive aporia of a period of Argentine sociopolitical history.

Sara's admonition to Alicia that "crying doesn't help" violates a fundamental Mediterranean cultural motif inherited by Argentine society: a belief in the efficacy of tears in the face of life's crises. Bathos may indeed do something for the soul, but it has no extra-psychological effect on the constitution of the social text, and it is certainly the latter effect that Sara and her colleagues are striving to bring about. Sara attempts it in the recovery of her kidnapped granddaughter, and the Madres try to force an open accounting of the disappearances of the *guerra sucia*.[16] Sara's observation to Alicia, which is uttered in almost pitiful terms in the face of the woman's lack of sociohistorical awareness, serves to jolt Alicia out of her world, in which domestic misunderstandings for women, including the melodrama of matrimonial betrayal, are handled with tears. Significantly, after this confrontation, Alicia takes Sara home with her and confronts her husband with the material evidence, in the person of Sara, that she now understands where Gaby has come from. This confrontation is a terrifying trope on the myth of the stork, whereby the dependent of patriarchal authority demonstrates that she now knows, not that babies come from Paris or from under cabbages (Hispanic variations of the Anglo-Saxon tale), but from the dungeons of the military police. With good reason, Roberto becomes violent and shouts at his wife:

16. This accounting has not yet fully taken place, which is why the Madres continue to be an active political presence in the country.

But, what is this nonsense? This Trap? In my own house . . . ?! What are you becoming, you wretch?! Do you realize what it is you're doing? What's wrong with you? Are you afraid? Do you want to get rid of the girl? You don't need pretexts! You don't need to give her away to the first crazy woman you find on the street! Get her out of here! Get this woman out of my house immediately! Right now! Get her out of here! (128–29)

There are two ironic resonances in this speech, one being the use of the word *loca,* the most prominent of the derogatory terms for the Madres (who must be crazy to defy the military regime, crazy in the way in which any dissenting woman is liable to be dismissed as hysterical or overemotional), and the other being Roberto's two-fold reference to the invasion of *his* hearth through Alicia's bringing Sara home with her. Alicia's willingness to proceed in this fashion and to defy her husband's wrath demonstrates her assimilation of Sara's implied injunction that something other than tears must be brought to bear in the solution to what has occurred; at the same time it is a renunciation of the feminine dependence symbolized by resorting to tears that move no one and vitiate any energy required to alter the social text.

All three of the moments of moral anagnorisis are played out against the backdrop of disjunctive moral allegiances, even when the third one, while confirming the irreparable moral separation of Roberto and Alicia, signifies a gesture toward the tragic ambiguity of Roberto's position. He is devoted to one set of values while corrupted by another, the two of which he mistakenly believes can be reconciled.

Puenzo's film has been received by international audiences as a powerful interpretation of the corruption of the military dictatorship in Argentina between 1976 and 1983. The corruption has been confirmed by numerous other cultural documents created by both Argentines and foreigners, the most important segments of which have been interpretations of the misbegotten Falklands conflict. Although *The Official Story* enjoyed an important level of success in Argentina, a society always more willing to see foreign films than national ones, no matter how good the latter may be, its greatest success was on the international circuit. It is in its international appeal, however, that one may identify a significant ideological problem for the film.

Cultural documents like *The Official Story* promote a moral disjunction of the world, a division into the right and the wrong, the good and the bad. It is a moot question whether such a disjunction is the consequence of a religiocultural system that it serves, in turn, to (re)confirm, or whether such a posture is an inescapable part of analyzing the power structure. As a consequence of the polarizations produced by the dictatorship, the opposition availed itself of every possible rhetorical strategy to characterize the violation of the constitutional institutions of the country, making abundant references to a long tradition of authoritarian usurpation; and the military government explicitly used the religious categories of virtue and evil in order to legitimate the process of national expiation of the sins of democracy, socialism, communism, anarchism, and so on.[17] Thus the period of redemocratization could not avoid beginning with these categories—now realigned; the new democratic government became the champion of social good and the displaced military the confirmed evil. The trial of the generals and other officers accused of the human rights abuses of the *guerra sucia* and the Falklands misadventure only served to underscore the continuing validity of such polarizations.

But social reality cannot be a Sunday school lesson in sin and grace inscribed in terms of the political process, and it became important for the military government's key spokespersons to refer to the profound ambiguities of that process and how the dictatorship depended on a broad base of popular support. That base may have been continually shifting, but it remained large enough to allow the junta to pursue openly and with a full array of propagandistic justifications many of its harshest programs. Viewed in this way, the belief that the Proceso involved a massive, desperate population held in check by a relatively small band of neofascist thugs, some in uniform and some in business suits, does not withstand much scrutiny. Perhaps there is no reliable way to gauge

17. It is worth considering in this regard Fredric Jameson's reservations about the facile uses of the image of evil in the ideological positions of cultural products, especially film. "Evil is here, however, the emptiest form of sheer Otherness (into which any type of social content can be poured at will). [We ought not] require our flesh to creep before reaching a sober and political decision as to the people and forces who are collectively 'evil' in our contemporary world." *Postmodernism; or, the Cultural Logic of Late Capitalism,* 290.

the extent of polarized thinking or to chart manifestations of its replacement by a more verisimilar thinking about the ambiguities of political realities. The important point to be made is how the disjunction between Them and Us has met another, external ideological agenda that is reinforced by documents like *The Official Story*.

Puenzo's film serves, to put it in brutally blunt terms, to confirm the modern-day versions of the Latin American Black Legend, the principal thrust of which is that all Latin American countries are ruled by ruthless dictators. This interpretation has been promulgated by otherwise artistically impressive novels like the Spaniard Ramón del Valle-Inclán's *Tirano Banderas*, (The tyrant banderas), released in 1926, and the Guatemalan Miguel Angel Asturias's *El señor presidente* (Mr. President, 1946). While more recent works like the Paraguayan Augusto Roa Bastos's *Yo el Supremo* (I the supreme, 1974) and the Colombian Gabriel García Márquez's *El otoño del patriarca* (The autumn of the partiarch, 1975) have focused on the ambiguities of dictatorial power, the aforementioned earlier works contributed to a view that dictatorship is inevitable in Latin America. This view is undoubtedly continuous with the postulates of the Monroe Doctrine and the need to justify imperialist adventurism. Since constitutional democracy like that of the United States did not exist in Latin America, commercial and political interventions could be useful in diluting the power of the oligarchy and its tyrannical henchmen. The historical record may well teach that imperialist interests in Latin America are only possible when they can count on the agency of a self-perpetuating regime like Anastasio Somoza's in Nicaragua to ensure the most favorable conditions for their interests. Toward this end, it is necessary to persuade citizens of the First World either that a tinhorn dictator is being displaced or that protection against a communist takeover is being effected, which amounts to the same thing, in any case, as a confirmation of how the Latin Americans cannot govern (for) themselves in accord with constitutional democracy.

The Official Story, then, internalizes, in its image of a citizenry held in thrall by a dictatorship, a horizon of expectation within the international spectator that it is proper to view Latin American republics as always governed by bloody tyrants. Puenzo's film may revolve around a classy woman like Alicia and show her moving in some very elegant surroundings, but once she goes out onto the street, the screen is filled with scenes of political repression that suggest it is the sole basis for the everyday lot of Argentines and other Latin Americans. Indeed, from this point of view, Alicia's personal development is a movement from the cocoon of protection provided the dependents of the regime's supporters to a realization of what dictatorship truly means. We never see Alicia being beaten on the head by a policeman, or horrifying scenes of films like Héctor Babenco's *Kiss of the Spider Woman* or Costa-Gavras's *State of Siege* (two English-language films produced for international consumption and reinforcing to a large degree the disjunction under discussion here). But public violence is transmitted to her in the way in which she is physically abused by her husband at the end of the film; and that kind of abuse, after all, may be considered a more effective signification of Alicia's full participation in social realities than would be yet one more image of a crowd being attacked by the police.

Again, it is probably impossible to determine the extent to which *The Official Story* supported smug foreign attitudes about Latin American governments. But what can be underscored is that the ideology of the film is unquestionably based on the disjunction between the good and the bad, with Alicia moving from a passive identification with the latter to an active affiliation with the former. The consequences of that transition in the period beyond the time frame of the film are left an open question. And what is being hypothesized here is that the disjunction forestalls a consideration of the ambiguities of political allegiances, though perhaps there is a nod toward them in the final embrace between Alicia and Roberto, while promoting international stereotypes about Latin American dictatorships.

As a result, it is necessary to contemplate a new interpretive proposition: the "official story" that is involved here is not the Proceso's assertions concerning the legitimacy of its authoritarian reformation of the Argentine social text, but rather the official version on the part of the Alfonsín government and its process of redemocratization that We were all terrified victims of the Them of the regime. This does not mean to imply that the citizenry at large consisted of nothing but supine accomplices or that the Terror fomented by the *guerra sucia* did not really exist. Of course the Terror existed, since it was even more an instrument of the *guerra sucia* (beginning with the sense of terror induced by that name) than it was a consequence of specific acts. The distinction being made here refers back, once again, to the imperative to consider the Proceso in more complex terms than the disjunction between Us and Them, whether promoted by the dictatorship or maintained by the opposition, implies. In this line of analysis, any complexity of sociopolitical analysis is forgone by the way ideological lines of force are set up in *The Official Story*.

Perhaps one of the most eloquent indicators of the foregoing is to be found in the confrontation between Roberto and his father, an aging Spanish Republican who settled in Argentina after Francisco Franco defeated the Republican cause in the Civil War. For the father, José (played by Guillermo Battaglia), what has happened in Argentina is an image of the Franquista fascist triumph in Spain, and he attacks his son for being an accomplice of the regime. As the other family members look on, father and son shout past each other in a dialogue of the deaf.

> JOSE: (SLOW, INTENSE, TRANQUIL) The whole country went under . . . only the son-of-a-bitches, the crooks, the accomplices and my eldest of my sons went upwards!
> ROBERTO: You're going to die believing that, no, old man?! You're never going to recognize that for all of you it went to shit. You have the same household appliances from forty years ago. The world keeps moving, it's going forward and it's going right past you who are gazing at the clouds! (103)

Roberto's brother Enrique, played by Luis Arana, sides with his father.

> ENRIQUE: And this other war, this one that you won with those from your gang . . . Who lost it? Do you know who lost it, brother? Entire generations of kids, kids like mine! Against them you won´. . . They're going to pay those dollars that were stolen from them. They're going to pay with their food, with their health, with their education. But you're right, you're not. What are you going to pay! You're not a loser. (104)

There could hardly be a clearer disjunction between Us and You/Them than this confrontation between Roberto and José.

It is appropriate here to say something about the figure of Gaby, played by Analía Castro. Gaby is a privileged and a precious child,

too Hollywood-precious for the weight of history that is chan-
neled through her person. Gaby, together with the trappings of her
socioeconomic standing, acts as an advertisement for the carefree
life a prosperous Argentina would like to attribute to its children,
colored by the moral attributes subscribed to by patriarchal authoritarianism. Gaby's socioeconomic status contrasts both to what we
learn about her pathetic origins (and, in Roberto's opinion, about
the perverseness of her "antisocial" parents) and to the subsequent
price to be paid, in Enrique's view, by the children of Argentina,
heirs to the consequences of economic fraud and the corruption of
national institutions.[18] *The Official Story* closes with Gaby attempting to sing along with María Elena Walsh's "En el país de Nomea-
cuerdo" (In the country of I don't remember), which is, of course,
militarized Argentina. As the constant point of reference to the
film, the wholesome innocence of this child acquires an aura of
tragic loss; she has lost her natural parents and now she is about to
witness the breakup of her adoptive parents and the destruction of
the secure world they meant to provide for her. The disintegration
of her world is in direct proportion to Alicia's process of *concien-
tización* (consciousness raising).

Certainly there is nothing wrong with a cultural document
aligning ideological elements in the disjunctive fashion Puenzo
employs in his film. There is no longer any necessary cultural reason to prize semiotic ambiguity in the way in which high modernism does, even if the practice of viewing the world in terms of "A,
but then again B" has left contemporary culture with a forceful
legacy of expecting so-called advanced cultural documents to
demonstrate multiple complexities and shifting points of view.
Postmodernism's stark relativism—some would call it radical
amorality—is not the same thing as modernism's affinity for teas-
ing out the ambiguities of human existence. The rather facile We/
They disjunction of *The Official Story* probably has more to do
with the dominant practice of mass culture whereby modernism
and postmodernism enter only as pale reflexes of artistic and intellectual fascinations, an arrangement that satisfies popular culture's
continuing demand for uncomplicated choices, moral or otherwise. The social text may be inescapably ambiguous, but there is
no reason to expect self-conscious cultural documents to be so in

18. See Santiago Kovadloff's eloquent essay "Los chicos y la dictadura."

turn. Indeed, one can argue that there is an inversely proportional relationship between the complexities of the social text and the transparency of popular culture, such that the latter is in part a refuge from the former and the proposition of an alternative understanding for the social text as well. A problem arises when spectators mistake a cultural document for the social text (which, to be sure, never comes to us unmediated by processes of interpretation) or, more problematically, when the social text overtly belies the process of clarifying ambiguities in which the cultural text engages.

It is now almost ten years since it became clear that a return to constitutional democracy was necessary, and it is not altogether clear that democratic institutions will survive until the end of the century. The fact that *The Official Story* must have an entirely different resonance in Argentina, and yet another shallower resonance among an international audience no longer engaged with redemocratization in the Southern Cone, is what makes it necessary to examine closely the disjunctive ideology on which it is based.

■ ■ ■

Passengers in a Nightmare (Pasajeros de una pesadilla): Documentary Limits

Documentary is a powerful genre of sociopolitical commentary, especially in a sociopolitical context in which the belief that reality is superior to fiction prevails or that fiction obfuscates the historical record or obliterates it through distracting narrative configurations. Under repression, the only viable, noncensorable cultural products were those that, beyond the "normal" way in which all cultural production is allegorical, made use of specific forms of allegory whereby things were not named as such. Within the context of the need to leave that practice behind, the documentary imperative during redemocratization had a special relevance. When such an imperative crossed with the residual modernist criterion of dense textual elaboration, the result, as in, say, the work of Griselda Gambaro or Luis Gusmán, was a text that provided an overall sense of the repressive crisis of Argentine society without yielding any easily decipherable signs regarding the specific actors and events of that process. On the other hand, it was evident that these texts were aiming for a different interpretation of authoritarian society than that promoted by a current national regime. Texts produced under the shadow of the dictatorship, a particularly significant example being the twenty-one plays that made up the first cycle of the Teatro Abierto movement in 1981, were committed to doing nothing other than engaging in transcoding practices. By contrast, a novel like Enrique Medina's *Con el trapo en la boca* (With a rag in her mouth), from 1983, or a film like Pablo César's *The Holy Family,* produced in 1986, both issued during the post-tyranny period, exemplify cultural production in which allegory yields to processes of synecdoche and metonymy for the purposes of framing actual events alleged to be consequences of a concretely given social dynamic.

The unquestionably heightened reality effect of film made it a logical vehicle for the representation of the military tyranny and for various ways of providing interpretations of it. The bulk of Argentine filmmaking during the period of redemocratization can be said, with little of the violence of generalizations, to constitute a mosaic concerning the immediately preceding period of national history. It is for this reason that the most privileged example of these products must necessarily be the television series of the mid–1980s, *Los miedos* (Fears), which brought to millions of Argentine viewers unadorned and only sporadically dissembling images of recent historical realities to replace the abiding assertion of self-preservation, "Aquí no pasa nada," "Ain't nothing happening here." However, literary texts like Maria Luisa Valenzuela's short story with the tropic title "Aquí pasan cosas raras" (Strange things happen here) could reach but a limited audience because of the smaller literary reading public, greatly shrunken in recent years from economic pressures.

The possibility of using a documentary format, especially as the basis for filmmaking, was, therefore, especially attractive because of the sense of present reality and the enormously expanded audience. That so many of these movies may, in the end, have ended up with disappointing audiences had less to do with miscalculations concerning what sort of movies to make than with factors that kept moviegoers away from national films in general.[19] Documentary priorities include making use of independently existing footage, echoing already established texts (whether authenticated or not), and making direct, explicit reference to signs of identity the audience is not just familiar with, but to which the audience has previously attached some degree of notoriety. Furthermore, it should be possible, without any network of allegorical transcoding, for the spectator to grasp how the action being (re)presented is especially eloquent in explicating the overall sociopolitical context that makes immediate and urgent claim to its attention—in this case, the period of the Proceso.

Yet, in order for the documentary to function as a privileged, unmediated form of access to sociopolitical reality, two basic criteria must be satisfied. The first is the implied guarantee—a contract between the text and its public—that known facts have been strictly adhered to, that, no matter how much an element of docudrama may have crept into the text (that is, the need to cover over the gaps of verifiable facts with a fictional speculation recognizable because of the circumstances in which it occurs, such as unreported private conversations or interior monologues), no assertion of fact can be expressly contradicted by available sources. With the setting of a sociopolitical reality that is itself resistant to interpretation because available information is fragmentary, contradictory, or spurious, the pretense of the documentary to furnish an internally coherent window on a highlighted historical moment also implies the coherence believed to accrue to the factually known. The proposition that an appeal to known fact may produce usable understandings of sociopolitical reality may well be an abysmal fantasy of our culture, but it (in addition to a legion of social sciences) is certainly what sustains the concept of the documentary. Thus a documentary can most effectively be attacked through the demonstration that one of its guiding assertions is a provable falsehood, and it is enough to isolate one such instance of prevarication to contaminate an entire text with the label of "fiction" in its most debased meaning. Once the text has begun to shade off into fiction in this way, there is no controllable way to distinguish it from the novel as a canonical literary genre, since

19. For the importance of documentary filmmaking in Latin America, see Julianne Burton, *Social Documentary in Latin America;* the absence of references to Argentina, in favor of more "Third World" examples, is noteworthy.

only rarely, and, it seems, virtually never in Latin America, does the novel not partake of the documentary to one degree or another in order to validate its claims on readers' attention, lest they be distracted by some other cultural modality promising more efficient access to "reality."

The second standard criterion that permits documentary to function as an unmediated form of access to sociopolitical reality is, rather than the advancement of too much information—that is, information that is excessive because it exceeds verifiable facts—the withholding of data. That such reticence has occurred can, most obviously, be determined by the access the spectator has to information available outside the framing of the documentary. Such information is already known or, more likely, provided by independent commentary on the film by, typically, a well-informed reviewer. Alternatively, and certainly much more interestingly, is the sensation on the part of the viewer of an incompleteness in the text, of an intersection of events that suddenly seems less adequately developed than at other junctures; of elements of exposition that, in conformance with the principles of textual production heretofore operant, should coalesce but somehow fail to do so; of a major nucleus of action that surprisingly remains less contextualized than other nuclei, as though somehow the structuring voice of the film did not know quite what to do with it.

These moments of silence or of uncharacteristic understatement introduce the sensation of an unacceptable reticence, since the text is failing to provide us with precisely what, by the conventions that define its existence in the first place, it has set out to explicate. All semiotic texts, no matter how much distance they posit between themselves and an image of the totally fictive, necessarily involve a pattern of selection and organization. They are constructed, that is, in conformance with principles of textual production that are, in their general working, independent of the notion of documentary truth. While the criterion of the latter may demand certain specific principles of textual production and necessarily forgo others, the operationality of some set of principles is a necessary condition for the text to exist in the first place. The problem is not to violate the principles that are put into operation for a determinate text—or at least not to violate them without inscribing that violation with yet another set of principles that attributes a semiotic coherence to the specifics of the violation, such that the viewer has a reasonable grasp of what is holding the exposition of documentary truth together. Once there seems to be an instance of narrative irregularity, like the damning intrusion of a wholesale fabrication, the generic integrity of the documentary is shattered. While it may be possible to install the now discredited documentary within a new narrative semiosis, it can no longer function for the spectator, be meaningful for the spectator, within the parameters of what is understood to be legitimate documentary.

Fernando Ayala's *Passengers in a Nightmare* (1984) presents many of the vexing problems of documentary filmmaking; moreover, it demonstrates the allure of the docudrama as one way of covering over contradictory factual information and supplementing the verifiable record in the interests of semiotic fullness. *Passengers in a Nightmare* is ostensibly based on the unpublished account of Pablo Schoklender, who was in prison at the time of the movie, accused and subsequently convicted along with his brother Sergio of murdering their parents. Many of the crucial details in the case were never clarified, not by the information available at the time of the crime, by Pablo's account, or by the subsequent trial. Nevertheless, it is obvious that the entire case hinged on the explosive culmination of events within what the popular press is currently fond of calling a "dysfunctional family." And it is equally clear that Ayala constructed his film around the Schoklender crime as an allegory for the corruption, violence, and dissolution of Argentine society under the military. As in *The Official Story,* the Schoklender paterfamilias is an accomplice of sinister business interests that overlap with various collective and personal projects of the military establishment, and like Puenzo's Roberto, Schoklender receives mysterious threatening telephone calls, is blackmailed, and quite rightly fears for his life, while at the same time fighting to keep a family together in the face of profound internal conflicts centered on the children.

An unmistakably political dimension of *Passengers in a Nightmare* is the fact that Schoklender, who is portrayed as coming from a typical lower-middle-class Argentine Jewish immigrant family, appears to be involved with covert arms sales in which other members of the Jewish community are accomplices.[20] Finally, Ayala's film turns to a great extent on Schoklender's homosexuality: his extramarital affairs, which are a major reason he is blackmailed and one of the reasons his liege lords in the military-industrial government complex are able to manipulate him; his impotence with his wife and her descent into a spiral of alcoholism; and his delicate relationship with his sons as a consequence of this entire overdetermined family romance.

Part of the enormous difficulties Ayala's film presents is the result of this pattern of overdetermination. Surely one could argue that it is not the film that is overdetermined semantically, but rather Pablo Schoklender's account, including the family circumstances that it reports. Yet the simple fact is that it is life that is overdetermined; and unless one wishes to create a situation like that of Jorge Luis Borges's Funes (in the story "Funes, the Memorious"), who is consumed by his total memory and unable to abstract meaning from suffocating details, then one must base textual composition on a process of principled extraction. Ayala chooses to set in motion a pattern of meaning that points rather bewilderingly in the directions of the "homosexual secret," complicity with the dictatorship, Jewish identity, alcoholism, filial rebellion, and an overarching inquiry into an institutionalized Argentine social violence.[21] There is little evidence to assert that Ayala strives in *Passengers in a Nightmare* for a postmodernist sort of fragmentary mosaic. Indeed, one cannot overemphasize how the filmmaking of the period of redemocratization is resolutely modernist in its striving for interpretive and symbolic meanings. The bewildering incompleteness of each of the aforementioned thematic constituents

20. The newspaperman Jacobo Timerman, who suffered torture and house arrest at the hands of the military, did not ingratiate himself with the Israeli government, which arranged his release and provided him with Israeli citizenship, when he wondered very publicly how the Israeli armaments industry could have as one of its favored customers a neofascist military regime devoted to the destruction of Jewish society in Argentina. Concerning the presence of issues related to the Argentine Jewish community in films, see Salomon Lotersztein, "Cine argentino: participación, temática y contribución judías—reflexiones."

21. Eve Kosofsky Sedgwick's *Epistemology of the Closet* is a brilliant analysis of the social control exercised through the threat of revealing the individual's "homosexual secret," a threat whose force is far greater than any truth the revelation may involve about the individual's sexual preferences and acts.

for even the most informed viewer may be taken as an index of the film's attempt to do too much with the material at hand.

Certainly, one can voice considerable confusion over whether the spectator is meant to understand a strict sequential chain of cause and effect leading from Schoklender's homosexuality to his wife's frustration, to his overachievement, to his collaboration with the military as a way of succeeding professionally and financially, to his wife's alcoholism, to his children's disorientation, to his wife's incestuous attraction to Pablo (in one desperate moment, she attempts to rape him), and to the sons' murder of their parents as the consequence of the accumulated indignities they have suffered. It should be mentioned that there is a daughter, but almost in defiance of the presumption of greater suffering for women at the hands of the patriarchy, she quite effectively separates herself from the family and appears not to have been involved in the murder. A classic family history like Thomas Mann's *Buddenbrooks* can make leisurely use of hundreds of pages of prose to construct a complex model of social interaction, examining with intense scrutiny each of the presumed pressure points, each of the tensed vectors of that structure. But a one-hundred-minute film, with the visual and auditory dispersion characteristic of a multifaceted medium, compounded by the viewer's inability (in standard movie-house circumstances) to "reread" a difficult passage, may be inadequate to coordinate so many intersecting narrative schema without engendering in the viewer a sense of semiotic congestion.

The principal thrust of Ayala's film is the establishment of a correlation between the Schoklender story and an interpretation of the dictatorship of the Proceso. There can be little doubt that the *pesadilla* (nightmare) in the title refers to historical reality. Although the film focuses relentlessly on the disintegration of the Schoklender family, the entire backdrop of that story is unmistakably the Argentina of an unmistakable moment in its institutional history. The figure of the institutions of military tyranny surface in the family romance in a number of strategic ways, first as the overall backdrop of the father's professional life, which provides his family with an ever more prosperous standard of living. The Schoklenders are a success story in one segment of Argentine society during the Proceso, that of those supporters and accomplices of the military who were allowed to approximate the pinnacle of economic power permanently enjoyed by those whom the military establishment loyally serves. The Proceso is also present in the details concerning Schoklender's actual financial dealings, especially in the party at the country estate of one of the financial titans—a party populated, it seems, by a startling number of human monuments to Aryanism, concentration-camp-tattooed Jews, and denizens of Argentina's gay community. And it is most dramatically present in the Schoklenders' party, which turns into a wild orgy, with the mother doing a bump-and-grind striptease (much to the disgust of the contracted artiste) and the three children departing in a door-slamming revulsion at the spectacle.

At the end of the film, when Schoklender wishes to separate from his wife and to support Pablo's decision to emigrate to Israel, she threatens him with broadcasting all of the information she has about his activities and his associates.[22] The revelations she alludes to concern, not her husband's closeted homosexuality, but all of the dirty deals in which he has been involved. Assuredly, however, his sustained involvement has been the result of homosexual contacts—despite the homophobia of the regime and its persecution of countercultural sexuality—and subsequent threats of blackmail.

Given the ground-zero presumption that an Argentine film made in the early 1980s is perforce going to involve an examination, no matter how obliquely, of the Proceso, it is amply evident that *Passengers in a Nightmare* provides a generalized image of the corruption of the military regime. Yet no effort is required to hinge the two spheres of the film, the personal and collective, on the concept of family. One of the dominant ideological components of the Proceso was the compelling imperative to reconstitute the Argentine family along traditional, Catholic lines and to promote the correlation between the moral health of the family and the patriotic integrity of the nation. Family and nation were promoted as inseparable facets of the same complex of human values and sanctioned by an interlocking network of human conditions, traditions, and institutions. Any deviation from the principles of the solidly constituted hearth was equally an aberration of the ideal of social community called La Patria, and the continuities

22. Eretz Yisrael was an important option for Jews, particularly young professionals, during the military period. Robert Weisbrot, *The Jews of Argentina: From the Inquisition to Perón*.

between familial patriarchy and political patriarchy, mediated by the ecclesiastical patriarchy of a pre- and anti-ecumenical Catholic Church, were so omnipresent as to be virtually impervious to ambiguity or confusion. The analysis remains to be written of the images of the family promoted by the Proceso and the multiple counterimages that proliferated and were, for the most part, routinely repressed. Among the latter, one might begin with Griselda Gambaro's grim novel *Ganarse la muerte* (Earning one's own death), from 1976, or Roberto Cossa's neogrotesque play, *La nona* (The granny), from 1978.

The construction of *Passengers in a Nightmare* around Schoklender's homosexuality and his wife's alcoholism (whether or not the latter is viewed as a consequence of the former) ends up promoting egregious stereotypes, in that gay identity as a legitimate personal commitment and alcoholism as a physical illness are never addressed. Instead, the film is content to allow the spectator to view these "conditions" as nothing more than topical, causal links in the chain of violence being considered retrospectively, in terms of the film's opening sequence of the blood-dripping car trunk, and proleptically, in terms of the concluding image of the murder victims to which it relentlessly moves. The film is homophobic only by what it omits, and it does denounce by implication the cynicism of the Proceso's persecution of gays, while sanctioning gay sex as part of a strategy to promote solidarity and ensure loyalty (by subsequent threats of blackmail). But in the final analysis Schoklender's homosexuality can never be considered as anything other than one of the elements contributing to the family's disruption, and it is perhaps in this dimension where *Passengers in a Nightmare* most segues into docudrama because of the lack of a verifiable record and the necessarily truncated information at Pablo's disposal. And it is also herein that a major structural aporia occurs; the film charts the evolution of a family story that leads to the murder of parents by their children, and it does this very explicitly through interviews conducted with one of those children, Pablo (played by an actor), with his answers to specific questions serving as the basis for each segment of the film. Yet it takes little effort to grasp how Pablo—not only as one participant-observer, but an especially self-interested one, since he has been imprisoned for the murder of his parents—cannot have been privy, either directly or indirectly, to all of the information that sustains the film's enactment of events. And it is with this slippage between what can be reasonably expected from Pablo's account and the requirements of narrative logic that the practice of docudrama inevitably intrudes.

But the intrusion of docudrama as the consequence of the need to underscore a relentless pattern of cause and effect is not what is most characteristic about *Passengers in a Nightmare.* Rather, it is the need to leave unresolved the agency of the film's central action, the murder of the Schoklender parents. On the one hand it is clear that the entire film works toward confirming the inevitability that Pablo and Sergio will murder their parents in something like a combination of revenge for the blind alley of their lives, most specifically the blockage of Pablo's desire to emigrate to Israel and begin life anew, and reactive rage over the hypocrisy with which the senior Schoklenders lead their lives. On the other hand it is not, in the final analysis, clear that they did commit the crime. One could speculate that Ayala, because the case was still in the courts, may have decided to stop short of categorically alleging Pablo and Sergio's guilt. But why make the film in the first place, if the self-censorship imposed by the Proceso must, once again, be duplicated in the very act of denouncing military repression? Since the courts subsequently found the sons guilty, it would now be possible to produce a version of their story in which their guilt is the unquestioned premise of the narrative, without any fear of infringing their rights of privacy or of risking prosecution for interfering in a criminal prosecution.

Yet, one might well argue that the absence of categoric knowledge (at least the categoric knowledge established by a judicial finding) is crucial to *Passengers in a Nightmare.* Ayala's film functions on the basis of the allegorical conjunction between the violent internal turmoil of the Schoklender family and the corruption of Argentine social life brought by the Proceso. It leaves in abeyance any discussion over whether the corruption of Argentine political institutions led to the Proceso as its most awful manifestation, or whether the Proceso imposed a significant higher order of corruption beyond that of customarily political realities. Are the Schoklenders murdered by their children as the culmination of a tragic familial disruption, or are they murdered by agents of the Proceso, with their children being convenient scapegoats?

The mother's threat to make trouble with what she knows about her husband's dirty business dealings and messy personal life and the individuals involved in them is ample reason for reprisals against her and her husband by undercover agents, and the last time we see the parents alive, as they are about to enter their apartment building, one of the infamous unmarked cars of the death squads cruises slowly by in the background. That there is no way of separating the deaths of the Schoklenders at the hands of a hit squad from deaths at the hands of their sons—deaths that in both cases, but for different motivations, occurred for enormously overdetermined series of reasons—can be an important semiotic strategy for conflating the assignment of responsibility for the crime to both a family dynamic and a political establishment. Such a conflation is even more eloquent within the context of the equivalence promoted by the military that the "sacred Argentine family" and La Patria were one and founded on a reversible synecdochical relationship—that is, the family is an extension of society as much as society is an extension of the family. In this way, Ayala succeeds very well both in denouncing the family-society principle of the Proceso's ideology and in recasting the question of violent dysfunctionalism on the plane of the hegemonic military dictatorship.

The problem with all of this is that, in so doing, *Passengers in a Nightmare* is no longer an example of documentary filmmaking in any acceptable understanding of the term. And it is not just that the movie has filled in some gaps by employing questionable docudrama practices. The very proposition that documentary be founded on a verifiable factual record, no matter how much that record might be strategically organized in the semiotic processes of the text, has been abandoned. And this abandonment goes well beyond the absence of a verifiable factual record at a crucial juncture in the story. Quite the contrary. What is at issue is not the lack of facts or the need to supplement them with conjecture, but rather the decision to move deliberately into a realm of strategic confusion, not in the sense of conceptual disorientation, but of conceptual conflation. In this realm the necessity of factual resolution is denied. An answer to who murdered the Schoklenders, whether it was the sons or the state, is no longer the point. What the film aims for in its concluding segments is not documentary accuracy but allegoric resonance. That *both* the sons and the state are the agents of the Schoklenders' murder is documentarily antilogical (unless, of course, they are legally defined accomplices, but Ayala never proposes this connection), but it is enormously symbolic as part of a program to assign the blame to the Proceso for the sort of fatal story *Passengers in a Nightmare* chronicles.

Certainly, documentaries are intended to project resonant meanings beyond the mere representation of facts; this is the allegorical dimension that is a necessary part of documentary practice, to the degree that it explains why the audience might be interested in the rehearsal of a particular set of facts. My switching of adjectives above from allegorical to symbolic, however, is meant to show the transition from the re-creation of a factual record that has a transtextual meaning—this one story is the story of many, and we are invited to consider in what dimensions such a relationship might be so—to a narrative modality, most commonly called fiction. In fiction, nondocumentary fact and conventional narrative logic can legitimately be suspended to enhance a more complex, more tendentious, riskier meaning, one that cannot be adjudicated via an appeal to specific facts. Instead, the meaning must be accepted only on the basis of a reality effect that makes sense in terms of how one understands the narrative principles involved, which in this case are those of the military dictatorship. The move from documentary to fiction in *Passengers in a Nightmare* is not necessarily an illegitimate one, nor even does it exemplify a postmodernist jumbling of generic categories. It seems to me to be a special case imposed on the particular factual record Ayala chose to handle and the overwhelming need to use that record as part of an interpretive gesture regarding the period of military tyranny. One ungenerous way of assessing such a case is to say that Ayala wanted to make sure the factual record suited his interpretive purposes, and the only way he could do this was by moving from allegoric documentary to symbolic fiction. A less personalized point of view might be to allude to the consequences of the need for filmmakers at this juncture in Argentine national life to ensure that all of the documentary evidence at their disposal render the maximum amount of interpretive potential in the confrontation of an overwhelming historical reality.

■ ■ ■ ■ ■ ■ ■ ■ ■ II ■ ■ ■ ■ ■ ■ ■ ■ ■

PERSONAL PROJECTIONS

■ ■ ■

Gerónima: Documentary Authority

One of the dramatic paradigm shifts in postmodern professional anthropology has been the imperative to develop investigative protocols that respect the integrity of human beings whose culture is under study, especially when members of the powerless are involved. Since it can be argued that anthropology, by definition, involves the study of the powerless by those invested with the economic, sociopolitical, and academic power of science, it is a question of an imperative enhanced in an inverse proportion to the degree of powerlessness of the subject. With its insistence on a sensitive respect for the integrity of the object, on not invading the Other's body and living space, and on techniques that allow subjects as much as possible to speak in their own voice, with the interpretive comments of the researcher being framed by a recognition of relative and contingent meanings, such an imperative unquestionably has much to do with the repudiation of the absolute authority of the interpreter as a consequence of invested intellectual power. In a so-called Third World setting, such questions have additionally to do with the application of putatively universal, internationalist models versus the formulation of autochthonous ones, as the tremendously influential Brazilian anthropologist Darcy Ribeiro has emphasized. Less a matter of denying out of hand the intellectual or the imperialistic power of the internationalist models—and, therefore, their legitimacy—which are responsible for a large measure of anthropological studies on Latin America, it is more a question of coming to terms with the necessarily blinding effects of principled scientific inquiry.

66

Such preoccupations quite naturally affect cultural manifestations that enjoy a tangential position with respect to scientific inquiry. One such manifestation that has direct links with anthropology and sociology—indeed, these two disciplines provide the reading horizons for it—is documentary filmmaking. Viewed in one way as a sort of illustrated sociological or anthropological text, the documentary film depends on the competence of its rather sophisticated audience vis-à-vis the structures of the human sciences both to engage the interest of the spectator and to make its exposition meaningful through images and voice-over. A documentary film "sounds" right because, in large measure, it echoes the interpretative strategies of high academic anthropology and sociology and their hierarchy of popularized versions. The documentary film is in essence one possible form for the mass-audience popularization of the social sciences. To the extent that such a continuity exists, there is a series of ethical considerations for documentary filmmaking that concerns the utilization and interpretation of human subjects, and there is a discursive problematics that concerns the framing and the articulation of the documentary's interpretation of the subject.

These questions come immediately to mind with respect to Raúl A. Tosso's 1986 feature-length treatment of the destruction by the urban medical establishment of an impoverished Mapuche Indian woman, Gerónima Sande, from south central Argentina. *Gerónima* focuses on Sande as a thoroughly marginalized and, therefore, alienated individual. Luisa Calcumil, herself of native Argentine origin, plays the role of Sande with a masterful assimilation of Sande's world, undoubtedly based on direct personal experience with it. It is a moot point whether Sande's alienation, in psychiatric terms, is the consequence of her marginal status—one assumes that it is; alienation is a socioculturally relative term—or derives from other factors such as heredity, prior life experiences, or even diet, all of which are, to be sure, ultimately social factors. The film leaves little doubt, however, that her condition is the consequence of her position in the structure of Argentine society—that of an impoverished indigenous woman doomed to extinction at the hands of an array of forces. In the course of the film, we see her at the mercy of a social welfare system that functions erratically; she is apparently entitled to subsistence funds, but these arrive only infrequently. The system also leaves her exposed to an abusive husband whom she finally turns against in self-defense, and it carts her and her children off to a hospital where the kindly staff cannot offset the deleterious effects of institutionalization. Sande suffers extreme cultural shock, and she and her children are finally allowed to return to the desert lean-to they call home. However, the combination of their poor diet and the alien microbes they pick up in the hospital leads to the death of Sande and several of her children. The establishment designed to provide them with care based on modern technology has, in effect, killed them, the culmination of a sequence of indignities that have converted Sande and her family into garbage-like inconveniences on the social landscape.

Underlying the rhetoric of social protest that serves as the principal rationale for a film like *Gerónima* is the inescapable fact that there is a series of enormous disjunctions between the space of the spectator and the space of the film. If the spectator inhabits the world of modern technology, one manifestation of which is the film itself and all of the engineering processes it implies, a world of the complex metropolis, of advanced intellectual and artistic accomplishments, then the space inhabited by Sande is a paradigm of what the former would call the primitive. Although Sande's world contains projections of the late capitalism, these occur mostly in the form of detritus: the ragged hand-me-downs the woman and her children wear, the scraps of sheet metal that are part of their lean-to, and other miscellaneous junk that litters the elementary desert of her remote rural subsistence. Such details are likely to be perceived by the spectator as incongruous or even offensive in the wilderness setting, and in this sense they mark less the intrusion of urban technology into the distant landscape than the profound split between the two spaces. Urban technology carried to the wilderness can only be converted into recycled junk because the wilderness is so much something other than the metropolis.

Certainly this process of spectator distancing can occur relative to the array of alternate worlds of the metropolis when these are viewed as either so many competing vertical strata or horizontal contiguities; this is the sense of metaphors like the city as "the urban jungle," the ghetto as a "no man's land," and racial, sexual, and ethnic cultures as "alien" or "underworlds." But in the case of the rhetoric of social protest, the pronounced spatial disjunction,

Movie poster for *Gerónima* featuring the principal actress, Luisa Calcumil, as Gerónima, holding one of her children. The top legend of the poster reads, "The conquest of the desert is still going on!," a reference to the military operation of extermination of the indigenous population in 1879. The legend under the photograph reads, "A Mapuche woman who was unable to withstand being uprooted."

in this case between Buenos Aires and the underpopulated realm of Patagonian Río Negro, functions to eliminate the spectator anxiety that so often accompanies explorations of unknown urban worlds (one assumes that they are unknown, since to make them known, in positive or negative terms, is one of the goals of a specific cultural text). It might be difficult to characterize the feelings with which any urban Western spectator approaches a film like *Gerónima,* but it would be safe to say that it is not likely to be one of anxiety. A predisposition to sympathy is, perhaps, what most leads spectators to documentary films, and it would be implausible to assert that the free-floating anxiety, with its tinge of morbid curiosity, that leads general-films audiences to pay to see movies about what they find repugnant in the social world would lead them to tolerate the rather flat (more often, this means boring) style that one customarily associates with the documentary.

In any case, a basic, complex disjunction exists between the realm of the documentary and that of the viewer. It is an acutely pronounced one in the case of *Gerónima* and includes Sande's situation as a battered wife. In this sense, then, a film like *Gerónima* goes a long way toward denaturalizing the metaphor of the film as a window on reality; the reality being portrayed is so markedly foreign to the spectator, especially a non–Latin American, that the proposition of the screen as a looking glass providing access to the unknown moves toward the literal. Citizens of Buenos Aires recognize that the "real" Argentina begins on the suburban side of the Avenida General Paz. Except for the provincial masses that have moved into the city since the heyday of Peronism and its support for such internal migration, they are not accustomed to being called on to confront the sociohistorically real dimensions of that fact. A film like *Gerónima* does so, based as it is on one of the most suppressed facets of Argentina, its indigenous population. Moreover, the southern indigenous population, by contrast to northern groups that enjoy a continuity with legendary cultures like the Incas, the Aymaras, and the Guaranís, are subaltern within the subaltern.

One could summarize the importance of *Gerónima,* therefore, by saying that it is an outstanding example of documentary filmmaking based on the true story of a Mapuche Indian woman the aspects of whose margination and death at the hands of social institutions are relentlessly pursued by the eye of the camera. The rhetoric of the film is clear, by contrast to a quasidocumentary like Fernando Solanas's *The Sons of Fierro* (1976), which examines the exploitation of the urban proletariat. But the film is neither strident nor biased, counting as it does on the judiciously framed exposition of the facts to make its point about the treatment of native Argentines like Sande. The fact that Sande's story takes place within the confines of one of Argentina's recent military dictatorships—she died in 1976—only adds a secondary resonance, since the authoritarian regimes have not been alone in the sustained benign neglect that Argentina's rural populations, especially indigenous groups, have suffered from.

An essential component of *Gerónima* is the conflict between the two internal spaces of the film. Tosso's documentary lingers on the details of Sande's lean-to, lost in the open Patagonian desert and battered by the howling winds of winter at latitude 42°. There is no attempt to garner facile sympathy for the woman or her children. They are suffering victims of forces of which they are not even aware; yet Sande is a survivor, and she is portrayed as meeting the conditions of her life with some equanimity, including handling her drunken, battering husband by dispatching him as she would any threatening animal. Within what the urban spectator must consider appalling living conditions, Sande is somehow able to keep her family alive, and such basic survival counts as an unquestionable point of reference for human dignity. Sande's integrity is built around her ability to survive in her own way in the world that is known to her, and the family quietly underscores her equanimity within that world.

It is when that world is taken away from her, or, more accurately, when she is withdrawn against her will from that world, that Sande loses the ability to survive. In the institutional context of the state hospital, she attempts to cope by struggling against her enforced confinement, the separation from her children, and the substitution of known techniques of survival with bewildering and threatening invasions of her mind and body by individuals who may be kindly in their regard for her but who nevertheless proceed with a brusque authoritarian power. Such power believes it has no need to understand where she has come from, so immovably convinced is it that it can offer appropriate care and nourishment to individuals like Sande.

The problem, as the film makes clear, comes from the sort of care and nourishment that such power has to offer. Sande and her children suffer from the drastic change in diet, three of her four children contract and ultimately die from whooping cough picked up in the hospital, and their mother in effect regresses psychologically under the onslaught of relentless psychiatric inquisition. These scenes of the film are some of the most terrifying, as we see Sande's confused reactions to the, for her, nonsensical interrogation of the psychiatrist, who is convinced that she suffers from psychotic alienation without ever seeming to perceive that her alienation derives from cultural shock imposed by her institutionalization. Sande is no longer marked by the half-smile of her former equanimity. She and her children are finally allowed to leave the hospital only after she has been indelibly scarred by her inability to adapt to the institutional wilderness and after her children have been infected with whooping cough. It is to Tosso's credit that he does not overdramatize Sande's conflicts within the hospital. She is never, in the snake-pit fashion endured by the American actress Frances Farmer, consciously abused by the doctors and nurses; she is not drugged or raped; nor is she in any literal sense restrained. In fact, there are some charming scenes of Sande sneaking about the halls of the hospital in search of her children, and she is almost successful on one occasion in making a break for freedom with them.

When the hospital officials decide that Sande is worse off institutionalized than she is in her lean-to, they agree to release her. But by that time she is psychotic, and it is not long before her children are gravely ill. Clearly, the juxtaposition between the primitive and the technological is not meant to promote a noble-savage encomium of Sande's ability to survive in circumstances that, for the spectator, are the most minimal imaginable. Rather, such a juxtaposition functions to underscore the violent nature of the technological as it invades the space and the person of Sande and her children, forcing on them a therapeutic program that ends up annihilating them as human beings. The unreflecting arrogance with which this program is enforced is, indeed, the terrifying dimension of this documentary, well within the tradition of similar documentaries on American institutions.

Thus, Sande signals another, much less lamented category of the disappeared in Argentina. David Viñas has claimed that the Indians exterminated in 1869 by the Argentine army in its infamous expedition into the desert, a massacre that secured the open plains for the expanding cattle industry, must perhaps be counted as the country's first disappeared.[1] But contemporary sociopolitical consciousness has paid little heed to the plight of the indigenous population, beyond a generalized realization that its members live in impoverished circumstances on the fringe of a basically prosperous capitalist society. Indeed, the so-called liberal commitment to social welfare is the driving force behind the "rescue" of Gerónima and her children and their institutionalization for their own good.

The depiction of the disaster of that gesture points toward the undermining of whatever faith the spectator might have in the beneficent effects of institutionalization, with an attendant undermining of the authority of the liberal program of social rescue via the incorporation of the individual into establishment institutions. Mestizo *cabecitas negras* (literally "black heads," the term given by the people of Buenos Aires to the people of northern Argentina of indigenous extraction) migrated to the city in enormous numbers. The migration, spawned by Peronist labor and social programs beginning in the late 1940s, continues to survive its original stimulus. Argentina's indigenous population, especially in the southern badlands, has always existed on the fringes of national consciousness, with little of the U.S.-style Bureau of Indian Affairs mentality affecting it. And it is clear that Sande's story is more of an isolated occurrence than part of a bureaucratic program of incorporation and institutionalization, which may perhaps make it all the more eloquent.

But the social dynamic underlying the last phase of her life— and it is intrinsic to the rhetoric of the film that she has not the faintest idea what is happening to her or what the stakes are— extends far beyond her closed medical file. It is significant to remember that Sande's story takes place during the military tyranny, and Tosso may wish for his audience to associate the "disappearance" of Sande with the fate of the victims of the *guerra sucia* (the ideological frame of reference that the Sande case calls into question). Nevertheless, the authority of urban medical institutions as they cast a shadow over the radically marginal indigenous population goes well beyond the parameters of the organized opera-

1. David Viñas, *Indios, ejército y frontera,* 11.

tions of the *guerra sucia*. Yet there has been the tendency—indeed, for some, the imperative—to emphasize that the mentality of the military dictatorship is of a whole with the founding and prevailing values of Argentine society and is not an aberration of it. As such, blind authoritarianism stalks every walk of life, even more masked in times of constitutional legitimacy than when it operates as part of the naked aggressions of tyrannical regimes.

Viewed in this way, *Gerónima* becomes part of the questioning of fundamental national values during the period of redemocratization, when the We-and-They disjunction fostered by those who sought to invest the military with all of the blame for two decades of repression was countered by the proposition that the sustaining authoritarianism of Argentine society needed to be revealed beyond its immediate and stark confirmation in the form of presidents in uniform. One might wish to argue that Sande's plight is too random to serve as a token for such a major ideological question, or that the professional deportment of her institutional custodians is too concerned to be condemned in the same way that one would wish to denounce gross stupidity, irresponsibility, or deliberate malfeasance for political ends.

But, of course, that is the point. Just as Sande is unconscious of the role she is playing in a social dynamic whose implications are deducible from her status as a synecdoche, so, too, are the establishment professionals unaware of the contingent meaning of the treatment decisions they make. The function of *Gerónima* as a cultural text is to make these connections that might not otherwise appear evident in the larger flow of daily life. As a social statistic, Sande's death would receive no or scant public recognition; it would only deserve newspaper space if there were something sensational associated with it. But there is nothing sensational about it; we are being asked by the film to view it as a routine sequence of inevitable events. But Tosso's film, as an organized text of sociocultural interpretation, asks the viewer to consider Sande and her health care professionals as meaningful tokens in an ideological structure that must be questioned if the unplanned destruction of individuals like Gerónima Sande is to cease. It is because people cannot be allowed to live their own lives without being "helped" by an irreflexively authoritarian establishment that Sande's story is emblematic of the plight of those who fall outside institutions that feel compelled to understand them for their own good.[2]

Sande's inability to reflect in a detached manner on her plight (at least, the film allows her no conditions for self-reflection behind the mask of her half-smile and her brisk manner) is homologous with the unreflecting conduct of the state's agents. Although they are permitted conditions of analytical thinking, for it is in such a context that it is agreed that Sande and her children should return to their hut in the desert, they are yet incapable of measuring the destructive force of their institutions. This fact is reinforced by the fact that Tosso's film provides no space for these agents to reflect on the implications of the subsequent deaths of Gerónima and three of her children. The correlation between these two spheres of unawareness, one of which might be considered natural because of the "primitiveness" of Sande's life, functions in the film to confirm a theoretical premise that social ideologies function without the individuals who enact them being able to step back and analyze their consequences, whether the individuals be health care professional or impoverished Indian women.

The aim of a cultural text is to provide the opportunity for detached observation, the dynamic that we have come to call "consciousness-raising." *Gerónima* proposes such a consciousness raising on behalf of Argentina's forgotten indigenous population, and it does so by questioning the legitimate authority of liberal, civilized society's social institutions, which are viewed as passively engaged in the genocide of the subaltern. Such a proposition is particularly suited to the nature of documentary filmmaking as exposé. One of the primary features of the documentary is the implied assertion that it is dealing with "real" life without the mediation of fictional configuration. Although narrative strategies may be involved, including a certain number of licenses to enhance the telling of a story in the limited time frame available, it is assumed that narrativity does not mean fictivity; and any unhyphenated documentary (as opposed to a dubious genre like the docudrama, fiction that makes a special plea to credibility) is open

2. This is one of the senses of Gayatri Chakravorty Spivak's famous essay, "Can the Subaltern Speak?" See also the comments by Rich, "An/Other View of New Latin American Cinema," 15.

to evaluation on the basis of its adherence to an independently verifiable historical record.

Thus, until demonstrated to the contrary, a film like *Gerónima* starts with the assumption that the audience will accept the basic truth of Sande's demise under the circumstances described and that her interaction with the government institution is accurately depicted. On this basis, the documentary validates Sande's function as a token in a way that fiction cannot, to the extent that the "creative" dimensions of fiction, especially contemporary fiction, may overweigh the specificity of individual and circumstance so that interpreting them as tokens is reductive. For example, what is Horacio Oliveira in Julio Cortázar's 1963 novel *Rayuela* (Hopscotch) a token of? One can say that "too much" is going on in the novel for Oliveira to be immediately translatable into a slotted role in the social structure, and if he is given such a role, one might then disdainfully assign an allegorical reading to the novel.

By contrast, the detached eye of the camera and the closing off of any opportunity for Sande to express herself beyond automatized behavior—even when, as she prowls the hospital corridors in search of her children, that behavior assumes an eloquent pathos—establishes the conditions for viewing the woman as a token participant in the social structure. The same may be said of the health care professionals, whose behavior is equally automatized (albeit more complex in its execution) and also portrayed with a similar filmic detachment, that is, with none of the various techniques that have been developed in narrative cinematography for enhancing the psychological density of an objective presence. It is, then, the conventions of the documentary exposé that allow Sande and the passive agents of her demise to be viewed as unconscious tokens in a social structure that, in the realm of the cultural text of the film, is presented for the audience's awareness; and any therapeutic results—pity, regret, repudiation, revulsion, social change—are presumed to derive from documentary exposé.

Which leads us to the part of Sande as an enacted role. (It should be noted, however, that the voice in the interviews with the hospital's psychiatrist is Sande's own, from actual recorded treatment sessions.) Professional documentary filmmaking, as a projection of the ethical concerns in the social sciences, must necessarily be concerned with how the role of someone like Gerónima Sande is enacted. Unlike fiction or the rather disingenuous docudrama, which is fiction pretending to be documentary, documentary is circumscribed by the imperative to transmit as much as possible the social reality it is describing. But on the level of the text itself as semiotic configuration, the presence of the camera, no matter how unobtrusively it is introduced, produces an alteration of the object. Furthermore, on the level of the film as a completed text viewed as cultural spectacle, reality is circumscribed—therefore altered—by the parameters of the general conditions in which documentary is interpreted and the actual, highly variable conditions of a particular documentary's showing. As a consequence, one must begin with the assumption that a documentary can never get away from the fact that it is a constructed, privileged, but still mediated view of direct social reality. Documentaries may experiment with the illusion of nonmediation, but their status as created texts, whether or not one subscribes to the narrower definitions of cinematographic auteurism, means that social reality has been reconfigured, if only by the conventions of narrativity neutrally rather than rhetorically applied.

In the case of the role of Gerónima Sande, who was dead at the time the film was made and could not, therefore, be used in any way to represent herself, the director's injunction was to have someone play the part in a fashion as faithful as possible to the already deceased historical figure. Calcumil plays Sande with what looks like such convincing accuracy that it is at first difficult to accept that Tosso has not used actual footage taken of Gerónima Sande herself. Both in Calcumil's underdifferentiated interaction with the nonprofessionals who make up most of the other cast members (one role is played by the famous Chilean actor Patricio Contreras) and in the totally self-immersed manner in which she transmits Sande's half-smiling integration into her routine and, for the audience, alien existence, Tosso's documentary successfully eliminates the star-playing-a-role texture that characterizes the nondocumentary (a texture, to be sure, that is now open to so much postmodernist camping).

Calcumil is Sande in the film, thereby leading to precarious illusionism that threatens to undermine the documentary validity of *Gerónima,* in quite a different way than would be the case if the part of Sande were being played by an actress enacting the conventions of the starring role. To the extent that we can believe Sande is actually present in the documentary of her own story, we are willing to accept the legitimacy of Tosso's representation of her plight. The documentary cannot utilize Sande to represent herself, but even had she lived, the film could not have used her to represent *unconsciously* her own victimization, since that would constitute an exploitation of her person; and her consent to appear would have been meaningless, since she was alien to the social structures defining informed consent. Since one of the interpretive dimensions of the film is Sande's lack of awareness about the social role she is signing, had she been made conscious of it so that she could give an informed consent, she could no longer have portrayed that role without assuming conventions involving the acting out of dramatic irony. This does not in any way imply a lack of confidence in Sande's adult status, but it refers simply to the way in which the film portrays her and to the way in which it would likely be difficult for a consenting Sande to have portrayed herself as a virtually psychotic victim.

Such a dramatic irony would undermine the authenticity of the actual Gerónima Sande as the embodiment of her token status. Knowing that Sande knew that she was a token would mean that she could no longer be an unsuspecting victim, and therefore the denouement of the film's story would not be relentlessly preordained, which means that it would no longer be meaningful as human tragedy. Or that it would be so only to the extent that an aware Sande was standing in for the thousands of other unaware victims among the impoverished indigenous population, a weakened proposition since she would have been shown to escape it by being the "star" of her own story. Of course, this is all speculation. The professional actress who portrays Sande does her best, with notable success, to make the spectator overlook the fact that she is playing the part of an Indian woman unaware of the role she is playing either in the social text or in the cultural text that interprets it. The result is that the ethical dilemma of the documentary is dispensed with. At the same time, one of the criteria for the fiction film comes forth, since one definition of outstanding professional acting involves portraying a fictional character so well that the audience forgets that *acting* rather than *living* is involved. But to see Calcumil as a stunningly successful actress rather than as the pathetic Sande is to undermine the virtue of *Gerónima* as authentic documentary. It is a moving film as much because the historically verifiable truth is being told as it is because of Calcumil's outstanding job of acting, with all of the rhetorical subtleties necessary to underscore Sande's *huit-clos* plight.

Perhaps I am making too much of this feature of Tosso's film. After all, there really does not seem to be any other alternative he could have chosen. But, then, the possibility of the professional enactment of a fiction and its greater attraction is the inescapable contradiction of documentary filmmaking and of the real-life appeal it makes to its audience, which is usually comfortably removed from the social reality being depicted. The real contradiction involved here is the alienness of what is being portrayed and the ever-present concern that no matter how the documentary filmmaker addresses questions of ethics and verisimilitude, what is being portrayed will always have the fictiveness, not of the narrative conventions from which the director cannot escape, but of the exposé of something so totally removed from the ken of daily experience, so totally on the other side of the sort of social and psychological divides created by phenomena like the Avenida General Paz. How to portray the socially alien is, to be sure, an ideological question, and cultural texts may well set out to address the deleterious effects of such divides in a society like Argentina. Certainly, *Gerónima* means for the spectator to understand that the authoritarian institution represented by the hospital where Gerónima and her children are passively abused is not limited to the Patagonian badlands. Subiela's *Man Facing Southeast* returns the same issue to the urban setting by focusing on a doctor-patient relationship that in its general configurations is not unfamiliar to the metropolitan filmgoer. It also involves an ironic redefinition of the concept of the alien both as it has been used in this analysis and as it is used by psychiatry. Yet, the fact remains that Indian women like Sande and her family are "out there," and an inescapable conclusion must be that no amount of skillful interplay between documentary authenticity and ethically sensitive acting will breach the gulf between the unconsciously played out social text of the subaltern and the organized cultural text.

■ ■ ■

Man Facing Southeast (Hombre mirando al sudeste): Ambiguity of Semantic Realms

Two facts about science fiction apply to cultural texts: (1) by assigning science fiction to the category of the fantastic or the (purely) speculative, highbrow culture does not take such constructs seriously, thereby allowing works of science fiction a freer range of ideological circulation than would be possible if they were circumscribed by the priorities of the cultural establishment; (2) the intellectual revindication of science fiction has repeatedly emphasized the ways in which it is configuring, in an especially hyperbolic fashion, the dimensions of immediate social realities.[3] The result of the interaction of these two premises is that such texts enjoy an immense popular appeal while (indeed, because they are) engaging in a systematic subversion of dominant ideologies in their aggressively pursued deconstruction of them via the outrageous conventions of the genre.

Yet such a deconstructive undertaking may not necessarily be in the service of a liberal or progressive posture that one associates with classic figures like Isaac Asimov, Ray Bradbury, Robert Heinlein, or Ursula Le Guin. Rather, as Susan Sontag has eloquently argued, science fiction in its heyday as a mass Hollywood genre functioned, like virtually all Hollywood movies, to affirm a reactionary agenda. The monsters and aliens portrayed on the screen were the consequence of a science gone amuck in its undermining of the plain, honest common sense of all-American types, who battled valiantly to reclose firmly the Pandora's box of nature tampered with by irresponsible and wild-eyed scientific intellectuals. The latter, of course, were but figures of all the political, artistic, ethnic, and sexual unconventionalities seen to threaten beleaguered Western society in the postwar years. Science had been hailed in the service of the war effort, but not as the free-inquiry paradigm of skepticism or in the defiance of conventional wisdom.[4]

3. The best theoretical work available on science fiction is that of Darko Suvin: *Metamorphoses of Science Fiction: On the Poetics and History of a Literary Genre* and *Positions and Presuppostions in Science Fiction.*
4. I refer the reader to Hugh Whitmore's brilliant play, *Breaking the Code* (1987), on Alan Mathison Turing, the mathematician who made the key contributions to cracking the Germans' Enigma code and to laying the foundations of the modern

One must confess that there is probably no principled way to sort out the constructions of science fiction in the service of a reactionary social agenda and the constructions that strive to frame dominant ideologies in a way that induces spectators' doubts about their legitimacy. It would be tempting to propose, as a rough rule of thumb, that those works in the Hollywood mode, because of their crass appeal to a box office success, involve actors fossilized in certain types of meaningful roles, the use of conventional scripts, with only timid excursions into the outlandish, and the reimposition, in the end, of a comforting status quo that was not really threatened after all. Life resumes as usual, with the alien crushed by the redundantly encoded hero of the normal, whose clear-eyed sense of what is universally right can triumph over the most repugnant extraterrestrial deviant. By the same token, those texts whose parameters appear to break with studio formulas can easily be taken to represent significant exceptions to a reactionary science fiction and to be gestures toward significant reassessments of social ideologies as represented in terms of radically reconstructed codes of science. Were it so simple.

The fact is not only must each text be thoroughly scrutinized in terms of its sustaining allegorical principles, but it is equally necessary to assume that the complexity of reconfiguring social ideologies within the conventions of science fiction will lead to a considerable amount of conceptual slippage, confusion, and ambiguity. Naturally, some cultural products might logically involve conflicting meanings. A presumption of integrity ought well to rule the most implacable critics, however, especially when they are resisting an axiom of semantic chaos, when they are approaching popular culture products aimed at a broad public and engaged in strategies to undermine that public's ideological assumptions. Put differently, there is much danger in using conventions identified with mass commercial culture in the interests of bringing about a reconsideration of irreflexively sustained societal beliefs.

---

society-controlling computer. Turing, despite his major contribution to England's successful war effort, was subsequently prosecuted by the state for his "deviant" sexuality and ordered by a judge to take feminine hormones in an attempt to alter his sexuality. Out of despair, he committed suicide. Thus the code referred to in the title is not so much the Enigma as society's norms, which Turing transgressed. The play underscores the terrible irony of how society was able to survive as a consequence of Turing's having broken the Enigma code.

The general problem—and it is not immediately apparent whether it is more acute in imperial rather than dependent societies—is that Thomas Kuhn's concept of paradigm shift in the sciences, bringing about far-reaching and perhaps awesome new ways of interpreting nature, implies equally revolutionary repatternings of society. Social conflict arises, however, when the latter resists the paradigm shift of the sciences, attempting perhaps even to deny the hitherto accepted primacy of scientific authority (which is what has happened with so-called creationism [anti-Darwinism] in the United States).

Conflict occurred when no quarter of science could any longer subscribe to a hierarchy of racial superiority, yet racism continues to hold sway in our society in ways that are perhaps even more pernicious than a discrimination supported by scientific opinion. It is, in this context, important to remember that the Proceso de Reorganización Nacional was, at bottom, coherent in its persecution of the three "Jewish conspiracies"— Marxism, relativism, and psychoanalysis—because Marx's, Einstein's, and Freud's shiftings of the scientific paradigms have consequences for social ideology. Dependent societies may be less able to gloss over such consequences or to counter them under the weight of research inconclusiveness than are dominant societies. The latter can support elaborate projects to problematize the importance of such paradigm shifts so that their impact on social ideology is perpetually postponed or they are trivialized as ever-replaced modes of intellectual consumerism.[5]

Thus, science fiction texts, probably even more so in products of greater mass appeal like the movies, must interface with a genre of sociopolitical allegory that is at the same time both immensely constrictive and immensely vague. It is immensely constrictive because certain conventions must be observed in order to trigger the recognition of a science fiction processing of meaning, and immensely vague because of the double axis of the problematical relationship between scientific and social paradigms on the one hand and dominant versus dependent encodements on the other. The fact is that it has been almost impossible for a culture like that of Argentina to produce a satisfactory science fiction literature,

5. Fredric Jameson, "Modernism and Imperialism," 41–66.

something that does not seem to consist of cheap or, at best, pale imitations of the enormous bibliography of materials translated from English. Alternatively, the expansion of the definition of science fiction to include some of Leopoldo Lugones's or Borges's stories or a novel like Adolfo Bioy Casares's *La invención de Morel* (The invention of Morel), published in 1940, seems rather a bit of indecorous critical huffing and puffing. It is into this artistic vacuum that an ostensibly science fiction movie like Eliseo Subiela's award-winning *Man Facing Southeast* (1986) steps.

It is significant to note right from the outset that *Man Facing Southeast* was a tremendously successful motion picture with Argentine and U.S. audiences (it is one of the few contemporary Argentine films readily available in video cassette in large rental outlets); it also won important prizes in both Cuba and Spain. The film possesses a remarkable degree of technical perfection and includes recognized actors like Hugo Soto and Lorenzo Quinteros, both of whom have considerable stage experience and bring to the film an intensity of performance one usually finds when actors with a rigorous theatrical training are imported into filmmaking. What may often happen is that the intense acting of such individuals may overwhelm the meager cinematographic skills of a director, the technical resources at his disposal, and the paucity of the script. But there is a felicitous balance of elements in *Man Facing Southeast* that has ensured it a secure place in the annals of contemporary Argentine filmmaking, one almost as secure as that of *The Official Story.*

Man Facing Southeast is the story of Rantes (Soto), a young man who comes under the treatment of a psychiatrist (Quinteros) in the Hospital Borda, Argentina's major mental institution, located on the outskirts of Buenos Aires. (Historically, the Borda is a monument to the scientific treatment of mental illness in Latin America, and its institutional roots go back to the turn of the century, when European science was making a major impact on the continent through the industrious efforts of Argentine social reformers.)[6] The backdrop of the film is the period of democratic reinstitutionalization in Argentina, with the attendant issues of the legitimacy of state control over the individual and the respect for

6. Hugo Vezzetti, *La locura en la Argentina.*

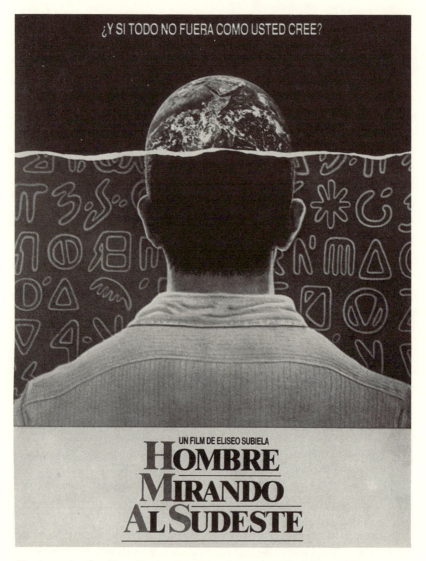

¿Y SI TODO NO FUERA COMO USTED CREE?

UN FILM DE ELISEO SUBIELA

HOMBRE MIRANDO AL SUDESTE

Movie poster for *Man Facing Southeast,* starring Hugo Soto. The top legend reads, "And what if nothing was as you think it to be?"

the right of a person to engage in unconventional behavior. Within these parameters, the film elaborates various conceptual fugues around the figure of Rantes as a nonconformist in an Argentina making the transition from fascist ideology, which is nevertheless still present in multiple residual manifestations, including the very institution itself of the coerced or only formally consensual treatment of mental illness by chemical and verbally therapeutical means.

The film engages various strategies to construct audience identification with Rantes, beginning with the passively decent and nonthreatening physical appeal of Soto's presence as an actor. He has just the right appearance to pass for an average nice guy, rather bewildered by the world at large but exercising just enough praiseworthy control over his own identity not to be "disappeared" into society as an insignificant cipher. Rantes is a common man, but he is the common man as a hero of gentle resistance to overwhelming conformity and annihilating anonymity. His posture aligns sufficiently enough with a vague sense of the decent that it is reasonable to ask the audience to be concerned over what happens to him in his rather dazed confrontation with a brutalizing reality.

Man Facing Southeast is constructed fundamentally around perspective on the concept of "alien" in its societal, biological, and psychological dimensions. There is no question that there is something different about Rantes, in both his behavior and his interactions with other individuals. The manifestations of the former include the spacey look in his eyes; the distinctly modulated manner of his speech, which makes him sound detached and unemotional; the exceptional skills he demonstrates in playing the chapel organ and in spontaneously conducting an open-air orchestra during an outing with the psychiatrist; his interest in the dissection of human brains in the hospital morgue; and other various tics and mannerisms that confirm his abnormality, even within the parameters of the quotidian psychoses that afflict the hospital population.

Rantes, moreover, exercises a magnetic attraction on those around him, beginning with the psychiatrist, whose several personal life crises seem somehow brought into sharper focus by Rantes's intense asynchronism within his milieu. Rantes's sway over his fellow inmates is dramatic; they cluster around him like planets around a solar axis when he alleges to be establishing contact with his extraterrestrial home base by facing southeast in order to receive transmissions. Rantes is visited by a mysterious woman who may be part of a former life he has abandoned in a schizophrenic fashion; but when the psychiatrist seduces her, she exudes a fluid resembling lymph that might confirm her identity and Rantes's as extraplanetary visitors. The texture of the film is a weaving together of motifs of psychological, biological, and social alienation that go toward postulating Rantes as a science fiction alien without ever categorically establishing him as such. Some of these motifs are drawn from the conventions of Hollywood potboilers, whereas others, like the metaphysical puzzles Rantes poses to the psychiatrist, are sufficient to affirm Subiela's analytical pretensions.

Thus the overall image of Rantes is that of an individual racked by complex multiple disengagements from the world he inhabits, and his death at the end of the film is a fading away, like a diminishing musical subtheme; the resolution is not destruction by, or redemption from, the alien presence that provides the coda to conventional science fiction films. In the latter, the visual ingenuity of the denouement, death-ray holocaust fashion, emerges as the whole point of the film, with a relentless building up toward it. In this sense, *Man Facing Southeast* is a stunning letdown, since Rantes's disappearance—he leaves behind only a box of faded clippings—is as mysterious as his original appearance. He has effected no impact other than a minor contribution to the accretion of myths surrounding the Borda and a profound moodiness in the psychiatrist. It is as though whatever project Rantes was supposed to be a harbinger of has been discovered to be dismally futile in a contemporary society.

Rantes's alienation in clinical or even popular terms is not something that is essential with him, not something that he brings with him from his other world. Rather, he is nothing more than a particularly sensitive barometer of the emotionally destructive effect on the individual of an alienating world that makes an individual like Rantes immaterial, both metaphorically in his successive dislocations and literally in his final fading away. Much more conventionally, much more "humanly" alienated is the psychiatrist, who is able to continue to function in the everyday world outside the hospital while at the same time being prey to all sorts of uneasy feelings, which he channels into his clarinet playing, giving the movie a final image for representing his pondering of Rantes's disappearance. Rantes is such a radical exponent of the alienated individual (not the individual who is intrinsically alienated, but the one obliged by society to view himself as such), that it is ultimately of no consequence whether he is literally an extraterrestrial.

Significantly, Subiela does not find it necessary for Rantes to function as a transparent sign for any predetermined ideological position. He does not bespeak moral regeneration in the language of the reactionary Acción Católica, determined to counter godless materialism with a renewed investment in the spiritual life. He does not embody the principles of social justice proclaimed by an assortment of political programs, ranging from nuclear interpersonal solidarity to revolutionary restructurings of economic relations in order to restore the dignity of the individual. And he is not a token of a sort of liberal integrationism that finds room for all persons in the human concert, no matter how bizarre their behavior may be from a majority and normalizing point of view. Instead, Rantes is a multifaceted negative pole, a circumstance captured by the idea of the alien—that which is separated and lies outside. He does not represent a series of societal primes to be discerned from numerous and perhaps even conflicting ideological positions that all contribute to the humiliation of the human being, to the "nobodiness" that is signified by Rantes's volatilization.

Rantes as the negative feature in a constellation of binary features throws into relief the various qualities that he does *not* possess—qualities that mark the dehumanizing characteristics of human society, which is here perhaps only incidentally modern and Argentine. One of the meaningful resonances of Subiela's film in the context of a redemocratized Argentina is the way in which that society remains alienating even with the abolition of the immediate control exercised by a fascistic military tyranny. The issues relating to the substance of human life clearly extend far beyond the superficial play of political power, no matter how horrible that play may have been for significant numbers of Argentines or for other citizens of dictatorial regimes. Such a proposal as the basis for organizing meaning in a film like *Man Facing Southeast* necessarily depends on the ability of filmgoers to establish continuities between their world and that of the film. It is not a question of a

continuity between the filmgoer and Rantes, even though his credibility as something other than a fanciful E.T. depends on Soto's
general Western masculine averageness, at least in his initial scenes.

Of far greater importance is the extent to which the context of
Rantes's presence—the other characters, the details of the street
life of the modern metropolis, overall values and deportment,
unreflective beliefs as uttered in the pursuit of daily social intercourse—corresponds to something spectators recognize as akin to
their own. This works far better with a film set in Buenos Aires
instead of in most other places in the Third World, because of the
general late-capitalist feel of that city, which has, in reality only
minimal trappings of a specifically Third World venue. The Borda
hospital, showing the fundamental decay that marks outmoded
and inadequate Argentine institutional spaces, is interestingly
enough the most specifically Latin American context of the film.
But the fact that the psychiatrist and those around him move in a
world that is fundamentally "ours" in the late twentieth-century
West provides *Man Facing Southeast* with a point zero of comparison for the spectator. Rantes's disjunction from that world is
also his disjunction from us, and, via an alternate and insinuated
triangulation, whatever there is in Rantes that may appeal to the
spectator's sense of identification with an otherworldly human
integrity is also that spectator's alienation from an alienating society. Rantes's dislocation is, therefore, only a hyperbolically dis-
tilled manifestation of our own everyday sensations of alienation,
leading us into flights of clarinet music like the psychiatrist's or
into viewing films like *Man Facing Southeast.*

There are, then, two essential ambiguities at work in Subiela's
film. One involves the suspension of the Hollywood science fiction film's categorical split between Us and Them, between the
inhabitants of a substantial earthly society (whether projected in
national, regional, or universal terms) and alien invaders who usually come to destroy the functioning unity (political, biological, or
moral) of that society. In some cases, the extraterrestrial may be
vice Christ, Christ having been a paradigmatic alien, the bearer of
a good news of redemption for an earth on the verge of self-de-
struction. But whether as a force of good or a force of evil, such
aliens are unambiguously defined, and the visual potential of the
filmic medium assures that the spectator knows which one is the

threatening Other and which one is the mad scientist's virginal (but nevertheless briskly American) daughter. By contrast, Subiela's main character is studiously underspecified as to the true dimensions of his alienism, and there is a sustained suspension with respect to whether he is an alien in the basic science-fiction sense of the word or whether his condition is more properly metaphorical vis-à-vis the humiliating dehumanization of our society. Yet it is impossible to ascribe to *Man Facing Southeast* a strictly metaphorical reading for Rantes, since Subiela invests him with certain conventional markers of extraterrestriality. The result is to suspend the focal point of the film between two essentially reconcilable meanings, a circumstance that may "enrich" *Man Facing Southeast* for multiple audiences while nevertheless investing the film with a considerable degree of ideological indecisiveness. That is, on one level *Man Facing Southeast* appeals to a wide audience as an apparent Latin American entry in an inventory of sophisticated science fiction with far-reaching social overtones; Rantes's Christ-like presence is a confirmation of this dimension of the film. But, there is the inescapable need to toy with obvious conventions of the science fiction potboiler, the most blatant ones being the oozing blue lymphatic fluid of Rantes's mysterious female contact and the main character's clichéd telekinetic capabilities.

But the ideological contradictions of *Man Facing Southeast* extend beyond the question of whether or not Rantes is a "real" extraterrestrial or whether he is merely a figure of the sensitive individual alienated by a dehumanizing society. The basic problem begins with the absence of any specifically assigned meaning to Rantes beyond his function as a reiterated negative pole. His ability to move food telekinetically so that an impoverished mother and her children will have something to eat is hardly a profound interpretation of an alternate humanity, nor is the talent to seduce a group of individuals into staring fixedly at the southeastern horizon. In terms of conventional cartography, Argentina and Buenos Aires are situated in a southeasterly direction, thereby identifying the immediate cultural sphere of reference for the film as either a current social setting or a utopia within the southeastern quadrant to be effected at some point in the future—say, perhaps, with the definitive installation of a postfascist society.

Rather, the ideological difficulties that ultimately beset *Man Fac-*

ing Southeast lie with the failure to specify what, exactly, Rantes's secret mission as an alien might be in anything other than the vague postfascist terms evoked by the institutionalized confinement in which he finds himself trapped and within which he ultimately perishes. Perhaps it is that Subiela, who also scripted the film, is less concerned with what a postfascist Argentina might look like than he is in underscoring a series of motifs that represent the repression of the individual in our society: institutional authoritarianism and one of its major handmaidens, professional medicine; conventionality in morals and the conduct of human affairs; the severe circumscribing, in order to render it nonthreatening, of energetic creative manifestations; the denial of the legitimacy of unrestrained intellectual speculation. Only by implication does Subiela match such motifs with binary opposites such as radical anarchism and irresponsible opinionation; but it would be difficult to gather those opposites into a coherent social philosophy, and the weakness of a term like postfascism is that it only articulates the going beyond fascism, but not what the other side might look like. Indeed, the term fascism, which is too often used merely to describe practices that individuals sense oppress them, itself has only the coherency deriving from the inner dynamic of an actual society; and its constituents may well vary significantly from one society to another as the social dynamics vary. Argentina and Chile under military dictatorships certainly manifested sometimes startling differences in the use and ideologization of repression (the government of General Augusto Pinochet, for example, never invested in the Argentine juntas' persecution of alternative sexual preference).

But the result for Subiela's film is a singular diffuseness as regards alternate social configurations, which are simply thrust out of view in the realm of wherever it is Rantes has come from on his secret mission. Invisible to both the inhabitants of the world of the film and to the spectators of the film, that realm and what it represents as a redemptive program for transcending the degradation of the human spirit can never be articulated within the parameters established by *Man Facing Southeast*. If the ambiguity over Rantes's status as a true extraterrestrial and the exact nature of his secret mission lends the film an aura of tantalizing mystery, such a blurred form of cinematographic semiosis also expands the film's potential appeal to mass audiences, who may have pronouncedly differ-ent interpretations of generalized concepts like "the repression of the human spirit" and "the degradation of individual dignities."

The failure to complement the representation of specific, known contemporary social practices with anything resembling a re-demptive program—that is, we see Rantes doing certain things, but we never learn what program of social meaning those gestures articulate—in the end marks *Man Facing Southeast* with an insub-stantial quality within any of the contexts it might be viewed. Unless Subiela means to promote a spacey detachment from the relentless indignities of Argentine daily life, with its heritage of authoritarianism and conventional morality, there seems to be lit-tle in *Man Facing Southeast* that concertedly echoes the themes of redemocratization with the sort of redundancy, transformational iteration, and overdetermined ideological statement that charac-terize cultural texts with a well-defined message to promote. In an apparent commitment to creating a general sense of respect for Rantes as an endearing outsider (rather than as an agent of an enraged and dangerous defiance like Randle Patrick McMurphy in Ken Kesey's *One Flew over the Cuckoo's Nest* [1962], also set in a mental institution), Subiela eschews the sort of ideological com-mitment underlying most of the films examined in this study. This does not mean that Subiela is lacking in ideological commitment or that he is disingenuous in his filmic version of contemporary Argentine society. Rather, what it does mean is that *Man Facing Southeast* does not depend for its meaning on an overdetermined ideological statement with respect to what a postfascist Argentine society might look like. The interest, instead, is in evoking abiding repressive motifs that beleaguer the psychiatrist, destroy Rantes, and, presumably, leave the spectators wondering about their own stand with regard to human dignity.

Man Facing Southeast is a very skillful film, not the least be-cause Subiela's cinematographic discourse ensures a very wide audience. One can assume that virtually any moviegoer is going to endorse the notion of human dignity, especially when there is no insinuation of what social reconfigurations are necessary in order to make good on such an endorsement. Few are likely, then, to feel threatened by Rantes and his gestures; at worst, some spectators might find his figure silly and his moods of detachment irrelevant to multiply defined, pressing social issues, no matter how they are ideologically specified. The result is a film of commercial success deriving in large measure from its being so nonthreatening as a consequence of its lack of ideological specificity. Were the film to juxtapose institutional acts of radical anarchy; were conventional morality and taste to be counterpoised by unmitigated alternate sexuality (greeting-card handholding by demon-conjuring sado-masochism, for example, in the spirit of the theater of Edward Albee, Joe Orton, or Harold Pinter, or, to propose an Argentine example, Griselda Gambaro); were something akin to an unfettered surrealism to replace circumscribed and sanitized artistic expression, *Man Facing Southeast* would truly evoke a release from the earthly thralldom that undertakes to contain Rantes.

As it is, Subiela's decision to couch his film within the conventions of science fiction, suitably tailored to a Third World institution like the Hospital Borda, can only end up circumscribing and sanitizing itself as an artistic endeavor, provoking in the spectator lots of fuzzy feelings of goodwill toward Rantes and, finally, toward his psychiatrist, but failing to marshall any sustained program to save Rantes, the psychiatrist, and ourselves. Rantes either simply vanishes, called back to the mother ship, or he disintegrates under the burden of earthly humiliation. Whichever is the "true" ending for Subiela's film is immaterial, since in both cases the film, and the consciousness of the spectator, is left with a void with nothing to fill it.

The proposition that Rantes withdraws because human society does not deserve to be saved has some virtue as a paraphrasing of the sacrifice of Christ, but such a conclusion cannot go beyond the pessimistic or even the cynical. What are, indeed, lacking are proposals to induce the Ranteses to dwell among us and to lead us from our humiliations.

■ ■ ■
South Side (Sur): Difficult Modernist Reruns

By the time Solanas released *South Side* in 1987, his *Tango, the Exile of Gardel* (1985) had already received international recognition. Made in part with French capital and invested with a singularly high degree of cinematographic inventiveness, *Tango, the*

Exile of Gardel spoke to the question of the enormous range of emotions associated with the recurring topos of exile in Argentine culture, from San Martín on down:[7] exile in the literal sense of physical separation from one's native country; exile in the sense of psychological alienation; and exile, especially in the case of Gardel, resulting from the discontinuities in national society, the spaces in which the individual becomes lost because of the absence of codes with which a relationship of identity can be established. Specifically, Gardel is something of a master synecdoche of Argentine culture, in his need to triumph abroad in order to be accepted at home, and the inevitable distortions in his cultural production—both the commercialization and the sentimentalization of the tango—in its alien setting. Exile necessarily provokes an incremental process of loss, most immediately noticeable in the form of linguistic decay, because of contact either with another dialect or with another language; and when the context is that of a totally hegemonic master culture such as the French, alienation becomes quickly focused. Solanas's film frames this alienation in satisfyingly diverse ways. It explores the various types of behavior that the alienation causes and the multiple strategies of lost Argentines to cope with it, always against the backdrop of the personal and national dramas that are left behind but that, as in Cortázar's "Las cartas de mamá" (Letters from Mama), can never be dispensed with.

South Side is thus a sort of sequel to *Tango, the Exile of Gardel,* but less in the sense that it shows the return to Argentina of the foreign exiles of the latter and the process of their reintegration than in the sense of dealing with the far more problematical issue of internal exile, in this case the exile imposed by prison.[8] Floreal Echegoyen, the film's protagonist, has spent six years being moved around from one prison to another in the Argentine southern

7. José de San Martín (1778–1850), the Liberator of the Andes, was forced into exile before the end of the wars of independence, and he died in Boulogne-sur-Mer, France. As one of the founding fathers of the Argentine nation, San Martín is also considered the prototype of the Argentine exile.

8. Reference might be made here to the enormously successful stage play by Nelly Fernández Tiscornia, *Made in Lanus* (1986), and Juan José Jusid's film version, *Made in Argentina* (1986), which deal with the problems encountered by an Argentine professional family when they return to Buenos Aires on a Christmas visit. This text is only one of several that constitute images of an Argentine family romance centering on variants of the motif "You can't go home again."

CINESUR S.A. PRESENTA:
**SUSU PECORARO
MIGUEL A. SOLA
PHILIPPE LEOTARD**
y la participación especial de:
ULISES DUMONT
LITO CRUZ
ROBERTO GOYENECHE
GABRIELA TOSCANO
MARIO LOZANO
NATHAN PINZON
INES MOLINA
ANTONIO AMEIJEIRAS
FITO PAEZ
LUIS ROMERO
MAURICIO KARTUN
Música Original:
ASTOR PIAZZOLLA
canciones de Fito Paez
y Alfredo Zitarrosa
Fotografía: FELIX MONTI Montaje: J. C. MACIAS
PABLO MARI Sonido: ANIBAL LIBENSON
Productora Ejecutiva: SABINA SIGLER
Productor Delegado: ENVAR EL KADRI
Una co-producción Argentino-Francesa
Cinesur S.A./Pacific Productions
Distribuye Argentina Sono Film

PREMIO AL MEJOR DIRECTOR
"PINO" SOLANAS
41º FESTIVAL
INTERNACIONAL
DEL FILM DE CANNES

Sur

**UNA PELICULA
PARA LLEVAR
EN EL CORAZON**

UN FILM ESCRITO Y REALIZADO POR
FERNANDO "PINO" SOLANAS

Movie poster for *South Side* featuring a crucial scene of reunion by lovers separated by the military tyranny, played by Susú Pecoraro and Miguel Angel Solá.

wasteland. After his release at the end of the military dictatorship in late 1983, he returns to Buenos Aires to take up again the thread of his life and to assess the loss in his small personal world produced by the devastations of the Proceso. Floreal's Dantean quest, centered on the encounter with his wife, Rosy, and child, covers the physical spaces of the legendary Buenos Aires south side, but more important, it leads him through key psychological realms of the past, both personal and collective.

I do not know whether there is a comprehensive study of the motif of the *sur,* both the South and the south side, in Argentine culture, but it is not difficult to point to cardinal points of reference, beginning with recurrence of the south side as a theme in

Movie poster for *Tango, the Exile of Gardel,* the first installment of *South Side.* The legend reads, "I'm twenty years old, and I've been an exile in Paris for eight years."

many classic tangos (along with Astor Piazzola's original symphonic tangos) that constitute a leitmotif in the film. *South Side* is the only one of the films dealt with in this study in which music plays such a crucial role, highlighted by the fact that dialogue is isolated and fragmentary. Ernesto Sabato's novel *Sobre héroes y tumbas* (On heroes and tombs) closes with a paean to the South as the new Argentine frontier. Sabato juxtaposes it to the history-drenched North, with its associations with the Latin American colonial period and the independence movement, which have provided both the heroes and the tombs of Argentine history. Sabato's paean to the south side also foreshadows a policy of the government of General Juan Carlos Onganía in the mid-sixties, which orchestrated a campaign to populate the South and banned bumper stickers satirical of this project, like "Subí, piba, y vamos a poblar

Patagonia" (Hop on board, sweetheart, and let's go populate Patagonia). Works like *Adán Buenosayres* (1946), which is Marechal's Argentine *Ulysses;* Borges's "Sur" (from *Ficciones* [1944]), a marvelous story of conflicting cultural primes, including the urban and rural, creole and immigrant, creatural and bookish; Juan Goyanarte's social realist *Lago Argentino* (1946), counterpoised to Alfredo Varela's "northern" *Río oscuro* (Dark river, 1967), both built around the pathetic fallacy of turbulent nature as a figure of social injustice—all provide significant examples of the southern zone as an expanding, mythic space for the attempt to repostulate Argentine culture.

South side here refers both to certain areas of the city of Buenos Aires, which include the *barrios* (neighborhoods) of La Boca, Barracas, Constitución, Nueva Pompeya, and areas in suburban Buenos Aires on the other side of the Riachuelo (the southern city limits), like Avellaneda or Lanús, and, in the expansive sense mentioned above, to the successively larger spaces all the way down to the southern tip of the country and the rugged wastes of the Beagle Channel, Cape Horn, and perhaps even the Falkland Islands as part of an extended conception of the lost and disputed reaches of the country.[9] I suspect, however, that the Argentine Antarctic has yet to enter into these cultural dimensions, although alleged environmental abuses by the Argentine military in that area may provide a point of entry into the cultural consciousness. Nevertheless, Solanas's film pretty much limits itself to the Buenos Aires south side, although Floreal's transfers between prisons and Rosy's trips to visit him, on occasion hitching rides with truckers—a motif from Sabato's novel—add the physical dimension of the South beyond Buenos Aires.

As a film that correlates a number of different cultural languages, *South Side* indulges in an extensive representation of the South as a lived space of Argentine society. Streets, buildings, vacant lots, a freeway overpass, and typical inhabitants are framed, not as a continuous backdrop, as would be typical in a conventional narrative film, but in strategic moments in order to relate the psychological dimensions of Floreal's specific personal identity to a specific Argentine sociocultural reality. That reality defines him, he loses it

9. Southern border disputes with Chile involve the Beagle Channel.

when he is *chupado* (caught up in a police raid), and he seeks to recover it as part of the process of reintegration on which the film turns. The South as a semantic prime in Solanas's film provides it with a title that obliges the spectator to subscribe to the presence of such a prime from the very outset and in every reflective consideration of the film. It is consonant with the uses of that semantic prime that both the realistic and the surrealistic dimensions of the images organize themselves and that the latter are the legitimate extensions of the former; the surrealistic quality that comes to predominate in *South Side* is, at least in the first instance, a way to enrich and to plumb the fuller meanings of the naturalistic signs that serve as the basis of the filmed scenes.

This surrealistic dimension is most evident not in the substance but in the placement of two of the dominant signs of Porteño culture—signs that, as befits their materialization in a hallowed setting like the South, are presented in their most traditional terms: the *conjunto de tango* (tango band) and the *mesa de viejos* (table of old regulars). Images of the band alternate with the lone figure of the *bandoneonista* (bandoneon player), portrayed by the composer and musician Astor Piazzola, who on occasion is accompanied by the singer, portrayed by Roberto Goyeneche. The band is the typical quartet of musicians associated with the most paradigmatic, legendary representations of the tango.[10] Whereas the quartet may be a more specifically "artistic" cultural sign, the old-timers seated on rickety chairs around a battered table constitute a familiar image in one neighborhood bar-café after another. The repetition of the ritual of their arrival, their order, their conversation, the general outlines of their interaction, and their shuffling departure is the stereotype of the continuity of life on its most intimate and quotidian level. The fact that these individuals are very likely all dead only enhances their symbolic, phantasmagoric quality. The conjunction of these two signs in Solanas's film thus provides two important axes for cultural representation: one in terms of the daily real-life context of the neighborhood gathering of café-bar regulars and the other with reference to a complex of cultural representations—complex, since the tango is a confluence

10. These representations are very much present in south side locales especially designed to attract foreign tourists, like the Viejo Almacén.

of music, dance, and lyrics—that serves as the quintessential artistic manifestation of Buenos Aires.[11]

The exterior trappings of these two cultural signs are eminently naturalistic in almost a picture-postcard way; however, Solanas moves them outside of their customary habitat and places them in the middle of the street, a windswept street that has lost its realistic dimensions in order to assume mythic proportions. Somewhat jarring is the fact that realistic details are still present, and both groups are backdropped by a freeway overpass that is symbolic of the "progress" brought to Argentina by the military dictatorship. For Floreal, making his Dantean deambulations through the streets of the South in the attempt to recover what the dictatorship has caused him to lose, the constant intersection with the two cultural primes functions both as a point of orientation with respect to his personal identity and as a source of information in his quest, since the conversation of the *viejos* and the themes of the tangos furnish him with a renewed impetus in his quest. By framing (stereo)typical images of the South, Solanas evokes an entire, almost ludicrously sentimentalized social reality that is crucial to one dominant interpretation of Argentine culture—a populist interpretation consonant with his Peronista commitments. Solanas expands those images through their reinscription within surrealistic dimensions; he uses displacements like moving a table and a quartet outdoors; concentrations like the windswept, littered, and fog-impregnated streets; distortions like the presence of the Virgilian guide, El Muerto (The dead man); and recursive techniques like cutting rapidly from a scene of mock massacre to a real execution. Solanas provides the details of a quotidian reality with symbolic resonances that lead the spectator toward a critical analysis of what would otherwise be thoroughly automatic cultural references lost in the texture of the overfamiliar. By starting with the familiar, Solanas establishes his populist priorities. But his process of semiotic supplementation through surrealistic images defamiliarizes the conventional and points toward the imperative for critical analysis.

The same may be said of the elliptic structure of the film, im-

11. See Jorge Alberto Bossío's study of the theme of the café in Argentine literature, *Los cafés de Buenos Aires*.

posed in part by the fundamental criterion of semiotic supplementation that overrides realistic narrative exposition. *South Side* is
elliptic in two ways. There is a high degree of fragmentariness in
the internal construction of the sequences that derives from the
conjunction of the realistic and the surrealistic. Scenes are constructed around an extensive degree of local color: recognizable
street settings; familiar buildings on the Buenos Aires landscape;
accurate details in the way characters dress, use their bodies, and
speak—all accompanied by a full inventory of references to phenomena and events associated with the seven years of military dictatorship. There is, therefore, present in this film the essential
structure of a conventional narrative based on Floreal's recovery
of Rosy (or her recovery of him, returned from the physical and
spiritual alienation of unjust imprisonment), and it requires little
effort on the part of the spectator to recast the evolution of the film
in terms of a full(er) version of an immediately recognizable plot.
Indeed, spectators unaccustomed to modernist filmmaking, if they
accept the task of seeing *South Side* through to the end, may well
only be able to make sense of the film by applying such a process of
recasting and plot extrapolation. One may wish to attribute to the
film a latent appeal to this process, made in order to enhance
availability to a broader audience than is possible with modernist
films with significantly less recoverable narrative plots.

However, returning to the internal construction of specific sequences, surrealistic details intrude to render problematical the
full local-color meaning of the scenes. Besides the altered space
for semantic primes like the tango musicians and the café regulars,
Solanas's strategies of defamiliarization of local color also include
the way in which the human inhabitants of the typical spaces are
used. Alternately, these spaces are suddenly emptied of people, as
though the film were taking place at 3 A.M. (probably the only time
when Buenos Aires streets are ever really close to hauntingly vacant), or there is the sudden presence of a crowd: a politically
motivated demonstration, the violent arrival of the unmarked cars
of a death squad, the forced march of a group of naked political
prisoners. Or, the sociolinguistically accurate exchange of conversation in the street among figures of ordinary people—a verbal
documentariness that covers the mundane affairs of life as well as
the political slogans associated with the period—is abruptly inter-

sected by the highly artistic tango. The tango is based on frequent topics of human affairs, but it may be argued that the tango provides a highly ideologized interpretation of those affairs that favors a high-volume melodrama of friendship, love, poverty, and death. Although the texts expounded by the musical component of the film may echo the real-life preoccupations at the center of *South Side*'s plot, the tango is a distinctive art form built around a simulacrum of the sociolinguistically authentic. That is, the tango is undeniably existentially authentic as an Argentine cultural production, and the authenticity of its language, style, rhetoric, and themes is a matter of the reality effect created by the ideologized conventions of the tango instead of by any externally verifiable accuracy.

A third example of the conjunction of the realistic and the surrealistic in individual scenes involves the omnipresence of swirling papers and swirling blue fog. Although these two motifs characterize the street scenes, which predominate in the film, they are present in an especially eloquent way when Floreal's uncle, a retired colonel in the army under Perón, goes to the War Ministry in the attempt to find information from another relative who is an officer stationed there. The modern halls are littered with paper and there are moments when the traffic down the long halls is overcome by the billowing clouds of bluish fog. Later, the motif of overwhelming scrap paper is intensified when the men visit a section of the archives in the ministry where volumes of subversive, antinational, and pornographic literature are being pulled from the shelves, torn apart, and tossed in the trash bin in a ritual of cultural purification. It does not require much of an effort at symbolic transcodification to see in the swirling piles of paper both the discarded remnants of a culture devastated from within and the traces of a burgeoning bureaucracy of official repression.[12] Similarly, the blue fog will immediately be seen as representing the clouds of falsifications with which the tyranny sought to justify itself. Presumably a blue fog, highlighted by the white lights of electrical illumination in the streets and in a building like the War

12. It seems that the apparatus of the military government never computerized its operations, as did counterparts in Brazil and Chile, and that the business of persecution still functioned in the Kafkian labyrinths of paper-based files.

Ministry, evokes the two colors of the Argentine flag, ever present in official propaganda. It is not so much that Solanas's film requires such gestures as the interpretation of these surrealistic motifs, but that our cultural formation usually leads us to an attempt to give them a meaning consonant with the prevailing sense of the plot. Whatever the symbolic meaning of the swirling papers and bluish fog is proposed to be, they constitute major nonnaturalistic dimensions overlaying the local color of the settings of the film.

The second presence of fragmentariness occurs on the level of narrative diegesis, whereby a spectator may want to flesh out the details of the romantic reencounter that serves as the basic plot of the movie. *South Side* does not present an easily recognizable narrative trajectory built around one of the many conventional stories of romantic reencounter, or present such a plot via a quick reassembling of the "natural" narrative morphology—that is, starting with the final scene and then flashing back to what leads up to it. Instead, the film is structured around key nuclei in the story, with a "natural" chronology that extends from the time of Floreal's release to the moment when he ends up once again in Rosy's arms. Tangential dramatic enactments of those events, outside any necessary chronological order, crosscut the chronology and represent impediments to the story's legitimate denouement. They include Floreal's arrest; his incarceration in various prisons in southern cities and the resulting psychological suffering and erosion of personal identity; his doubts about Rosy's faithfulness, which are highlighted by her refuge from the terrible loneliness in the arms of someone else; and the sense of destruction Floreal experiences when he returns to the *barrio* and, led by El Muerto, sees how much everything has changed, materially as well as spiritually. The cutting back and forth between pertinent moments in the core plot and the tangential representations of the present are instances of the impediments in the realization of an expected plot evolution that provides a fundamental distance from conventional filmic narrativity. It is this distance that allows one to speak of *South Side* as an example of modernist cinematography. Moreover, the fact that the transequential ellipses are augmented by the conjunction of realist and surrealistic elements within individual scenes and sequences can only serve to enhance the quality of defamiliarization that envelops what could otherwise be taken as a conventional story about romantic reencounter during a certain, dreadful time in Argentine history.

As a consequence of the way in which Solanas strives for a modernist, nonnarrative configuration for his film, there is the foregrounding of a constellation of sociocultural motifs that make *South Side* immediately recognizable as an ideological document and as a text in which the love story motif is inscribed within specific sociopolitical parameters. Certainly, the cultural themes and local color of the south side together constitute one way in which Floreal and Rosy's story is framed by specific conceptual parameters. Solanas's Peronista commitments are clearly evident in references to labor unrest, specifically as regards the meat packers' union (the workplaces of the members of meat packers' unions are prominent on the south side of Buenos Aires), and to various political movements that sought before, during, and after the dictatorship to vindicate the interests of union members and the social class they represented. These strands of Argentine social history are brought together in the form the Proyecto Sur, a clandestine operation that undertakes to chronicle fifty years of exploitation of Argentina by foreign interests and their local agents.

By gathering documentation referring to prominent individuals and organizations whose work is brought together in the Proyecto Sur, its director, Don Emilio, underscores an ambitious countercultural enterprise to provide an alternative to the official history of the Proceso. When Don Emilio visits the War Ministry, the nightmare scene of cultural destruction in the archives evokes an operation specifically against the Proyecto Sur and its subversive intent. Don Emilio counters the authoritarian self-sufficiency of the military spokesman by asserting, "If you don't understand the South, it's because you're from the North"—an assertion that juxtaposes South, as an authentic, national, human space, and North, as the space of pretentious and ultimately oppressive metropolitanism, in the sense referred to at the beginning of this discussion. His assertion also bespeaks the difference between the south side of the city, where the proletariat is concentrated, and the north side, including Palermo, Barrio Norte, and the northern elite bedroom communities like San Isidro, La Lucila, Martínez, and Olivos, the location of the president's residence, inhabited by a uniformed tyrant; and in the larger terms of national interests and foreign exploitation, it bespeaks the difference between the Southern Hemisphere and the Northern Hemisphere, the latter the seat of power of the British predators, whose operations fill the early files of the Proyecto Sur, and of the United States military-industrial complex, primarily responsible for the current dictatorship.

The image of the Proyecto Sur and its multiplicity of sociocultural details serves as a convenient axiological point of reference for Solanas's film. Solanas is able, on a popular level, to satisfy his Peronista commitments by evoking motifs that are as much a part of Argentine culture as they are specifically Peronista. Indeed, a large segment of Peronista populism started out by expropriating popular motifs and, conversely, deeply embedding its contributions in a comprehensive Argentine popular culture. For example, the figure of Eva Perón now extends far beyond Peronism as such.[13] And yet, as far as a higher political culture is concerned, Solanas avoids any reference to actual Peronista platforms of the period by focusing attention on the fictional, mythic Proyecto Sur. One ventures to say that this is owing less to Solanas's wishes to eschew getting involved in the programs of the Peronista leadership than to his desire to displace the naturalistic—actual political priorities—with the modernistic, a symbolic embodiment that need not be bothered with policy shifts, for example, between the times of the production and release of the film and between the release and subsequent viewings.

In larger terms, the ideological commitment of Solanas's film, like that of the majority of the texts from the period of redemocratization, revolves around the recovery of a legitimate human dignity in the face of the human rights violations of the military dictatorship, here given specific narrative form in the story of Floreal and Rosy's relationship. El Muerto, as he sends Floreal off finally to embrace Rosy, freed at last of the impediments that have kept them apart even after Floreal's release from prison and return to the *barrio,* affirms, "I am your memory." With this statement, El Muerto articulates how the film has centered on, via Floreal and Rosy's recovery of each other, the recovery of fundamental human values like a respect for life, interpersonal love and affective friend-

13. Julie M. Taylor, *Eva Perón: The Myths of a Woman.*

ship, communal solidarity, and the sense of self-worth that enables
one to value others. Within this context is projected the recovery
also—in a voyage of literal return from the other South, that of the
military prisons—of a specific cultural space identified as the Porteño Sur. Within this context, too, certain topoi punctuate the
film—topoi like "Cuánto hemos cambiado en estos años"; "Cuántas
cosas murieron en estos años"; "Lo único que tenemos es decir
no"; "Es muy dura la vuelta"; "[Estas son] historias de los años
ausentes" (How we've changed in these years; How many things
died in these years; The only thing we have is to say no; The change
is very hard; These are stories of absent years). Such punctuation
points serve as fundamental ethical principles that may have a specifically programmatic political importance, and their importance
is essentially highlighted against the emergence from a nightmare of
repression that the film is all about.

Solanas's deployment of modernist dimensions in *South Side,*
therefore, substitutes for a conventionally recognizable narrative a
series of cinematographic nuclei and strategies of elliptic sequences
and fragmented fragmentary internal scenes. Solanas's film amply
validates Rodowick's characterization of the countercinema: "[T]he
text of countercinema is marked by its interiorization and critical
interrogation of the codes of Hollywood narrative cinema—for
example, narrative transitivity (linear and teleological exposition);
emotional identification with the characters and diegesis; repre-
sentational transparency (masking of the means of production); a
singular, unified, and homogenous diegetic space; textual closure
presupposing a self-contained fiction—all of which are designed
to yield a narrative pleasure aimed at pacifying the spectator."[14]

The question that must now be raised is what is the semiotic
value to be associated with such a movement away from the more
properly narrative structure that characterizes the overwhelming
majority of the films examined in this study. One must presume
that there is a specific reason for all the bluish fog and wasteland
winds in *South Side,* something beyond merely an investment in
artistic trendiness that will confirm the ability of Argentine moviemaking to be as stylishly modernist as the French or whoever. If
there is not the goal of inducing the sort of critical analysis envi-

14. Rodowick, *The Crisis of Political Modernism,* 52–53.

sioned by a politicized modernist aesthetic, then there can be little interest beyond the curious in the features of Solanas's film that I have been describing thus far.

From the outset Solanas would want to orient the spectator toward an analysis of the enormous difficulties of social reintegration, from the perspectives of both Floreal and Rosy. The transition from tyranny to democracy and the suspension of the structures of repression such that Floreal can be released do not automatically presage the uncomplicated recovery of the multiple personal and collective meanings of the South as a figure for an authentic national life. Surely the presence of El Muerto, as much a voice from Floreal's lost past as an omnipresent sign of the devastation of the Proceso, is still inside society to the extent that his person intersects with the open wound of Floreal's memory. But his presence is also outside society inasmuch as his death allows him to reflect back on it in a wild and uncontrolled transgressive manner because he has nothing further to lose. Thus he is a point of entry into the reflective process that Solanas's modernist gesture would propose to stimulate. Yet, beyond a meditation on the ways in which transition and reintegration must be much more traumatic than the slogans of redemocratization would have the citizenry believe, *South Side* cannot have as its focus a critique of either the ethics of the Proceso itself or the ethics of the conduct of the spectrum of victims whose psychological humiliations and physical suffering provide the basic plot impetus—clearly not the latter, since their humble tokenism, within a Peronista mystique and other ideological premises concerning decent citizens, necessarily places them beyond reproach by the very nature of their victimization.

It is for this reason that not even Rosy's affective relationship with the foreigner can in any proper sense of the term be called an example of a bourgeois affair of unfaithfulness. Rosy's need for Roberto is thus understood as an index of the horrendous solitude imposed on her by Floreal's enforced separation and the difficulties imposed on communication between them by the circumstances of imprisonment, a situation that becomes critical when Floreal's doubts lead him to refuse to see Rosy during the periods of visitation permitted by the authorities. And, in the same vein, no reflection is required on the depredations of the Proceso, since that is the dominant working proposition of the film, the unimpeach-able human and social truth in terms of which everything else makes sense. Any reservation about the legitimacy of this truth would, quite simply, render the entire film semantically inoperant.

Finally, Solanas cannot allow himself any conceptual space for the questioning of Peronista conduct before, during, and after the Proceso. Unlike Héctor Olivera's *A Funny Dirty Little War,* where the tragic follies deriving from the internal contradictions of Peron-ism in the early 1970s are the motivating force of the text, *South Side,* by virtue of the way in which political ideology is framed in mythic terms, through the symbolic investment in the fictitious Proyecto Sur, places itself beyond—or sidesteps—the nitty-gritty of partisan politics and the real dramas of human fallibility that politics inevitably engenders. Since the semiosis of *South Side* pre-cludes any opportunity for the examination of human weaknesses, the critical analysis toward which the processes of defamiliariza-tion and foregrounding point cannot signal such a dimension. That dimension is often present in what we have come to consider the subtler varieties of narrative fictions and is precisely what we find present in a film like Subiela's *Man Facing Southeast,* with its em-phasis on personal ethics in the context of institutional psychiatry.

And so we return to Rodowick:

> Codified representational norms certainly constrain meaning at the level of signification. But to the extent that texts are productive of contradiction, it is necessary for political criticism to recognize the way these contradictions may be contained or dissimulated by modes of consumption or interpretation extrinsic to the text. Texts may be inserted into reading conjunctures that either complete their meanings and rationalize their contradictions, or that identify, analyze, and chal-lenge those contradictions. This is precisely the terrain on which a political criticism will operate as an activity of reading.
>
> Two conclusions may be drawn from this critique in the context of my discussion of the crisis of political modernism. First, once the structural integrity and self-sufficiency of the text are questioned, once the text is no longer conceived under the philosophemes of iden-tity and presence, any notion of the text's unilateral determination of subjectivity is proven inadequate. Despite the insistence within the discourse of political modernism on the centrality of a theory of the subject, it is the centrality of questions of the aesthetic text and of aesthetic form that have predominated. Moreover, having made the question of aesthetic form decisive for the study of ideology, the dis-

course of political modernism produces a notion of text that sublates the question of the subject, rendering it as the specular simulacrum of the text's own image.

Second, political modernism's particular delimitation of the text as a site of "political" activity can now be understood as naive. Once the criteria devolving from the formal self-identity of the text are challenged, the required epistemological judgment—which decides between ideological and theoretical or illusionist/idealist and materialist films—is rendered inconclusive. . . . A text is not an event but a function, determined by its historical placement within a mode of consumption or interpretation.[15]

The nagging question with which one is left in the case of Solanas's film, with its clear and evident commitment to a political modernism in cinematography, is what exactly can be its function as a site of political activity. Leaving aside any desire to assess how much *South Side* is modernist—I insist that it is, as is also the earlier *Tango, the Exile of Gardel*—and leaving aside an assessment of how competent that modernism is (constituents like the bluish fog unintentionally become self-parodies, but otherwise the film strikes this viewer as artistically superior, certainly well above the norm of the other films produced in Argentina during the period 1983–1988), a careful consideration of the gestures toward a cinematographic political modernism renders a rather thin balance indeed. It is difficult to suggest what the contradictions the film could have dealt with might be, whether in ethical motivations of the characters, the cultural motifs of Peronista populism contained in the master synecdoche of the South, or the conventionalism of the plot formula of lovers who are star-crossed by the military dictatorship and who are finally reunited after undergoing a series of tests worthy of the morphology of the most traditional folktale.

Furthermore, identity and presence cannot even begin to be questioned by *South Side,* unless it is the political identity of Peronism, which is suspended when it is not subordinated to the populist myth of the South. The protagonists of the film are simply no more than grammatical functions in a narrative syntax of romantic reunion. In this way the problematics of the subject Rodowick recognizes as deriving from political modernism cannot arise in *South Side* because the characters are little more than con-

15. Ibid., 286–87.

venient populist stereotypes. The conclusion emerges as inevitable that, as cinematographic artifice, *South Side* manifests all of the resources ultimately at the disposal of the Argentine filmmaker who has garnered unto himself an international following, whereas the central core around which those resources are marshaled is, rather than absent or contradictory or problematical, quite simply hollow.[16] From which one concludes that the modes of consumption or interpretation extrinsic to the text remain a preaching to the converted, which has always been the goal of political filmmaking in the basest sense of the term.

16. See Jameson, "Modernism and Imperialism," regarding the limitations of pertinence to Third World cultural contexts of the practices of First World modernism.

■ ■ ■ ■ ■ ■ ■ ■ III ■ ■ ■ ■ ■ ■ ■ ■ ■

LOVE STORIES

■ ■ ■

The Dogs of Night (*Perros de la noche*): **Structural and Personal Violence**

There can be no backing away from the fact that the period of the so-called Proceso de Reorganización Nacional inspired by the military must count as the most violent and repressive phase of contemporary Argentine history. The consequences of the processes of repression, of persecution and oppression, and of a general social climate of fear and mistrust, all in the name of fighting the nebulous specter of an alleged left-wing subversion, are incalculable. Democratic culture in the wake of the Proceso has had implicitly as one of its principal tasks the chronicling of these consequences, and it is safe to predict that this type of interpretive undertaking will last for some time, unless it is interrupted and submerged by a new period of dictatorial tyranny.

One of the consequences of the Proceso, on the level of textual production, is an interpretive undertaking whereby works, especially those that bear any immediate resemblance to documentary social reality, are understood to deal with the dynamic of violence underlying and sustained by the military regimes. Additionally, in terms of what is perceived to be semiotically unmediated social content, individual and collective behavior as it is constructed fictionally is understood to bear some sort of symmetrical or proportional relationship to prevailing social circumstances. In short, the action of the text is an allegory, to one degree or another transparent, of the real, historical world. Since all cultural production may be read in these allegorical terms, the emphasis here lies with the avowal that the real, historical world is being exposed in the most immediate fashion possible and that the only reasonable de-codification of the text is in terms of a generalized sense of said prevailing social circumstances.

Certainly, this dual process has operated in recent Argentine culture. Writers have felt the need to address what are perceived to be the devastating consequences of authoritarian dictatorship and to offer a discourse to counteract the duplicitous official one: fiction will provide a truer image of society than the version of actual events provided by an illegitimate authority. But also, repression and this response to it by a contestatorial cultural production will combine to encourage a reading of culture whereby all documents will be interpreted as dealing with immediate historical conditions of such overwhelming proportions that there is no way to escape the grip they hold on even the most minimally committed social consciousness.

It is primarily owing to this circuit of cultural production and textual interpretation that a large number of works could be produced during the authoritarian regime that sought unreservedly to deny its destructive consequences. While it is true that a novel like Enrique Medina's *The Dogs of Night* (1977) could not survive the mechanism of cultural censorship (like most of Medina's literary production of the period, *The Dogs of Night* was promptly banned after its publication), copies of the novel circulated clandestinely and enough was known about this and other of Medina's works, as well as the writings of other authors who suffered such persecutions, that one may speak of an adjacent stratum of cultural opposition, even though actual examples of it were not immediately apparent in public spaces. After the return to democracy, when novels like *The Dogs of Night* could be brought back into print and commercially distributed, it was only natural that it served as one of the texts reinterpreted by the newfound democratic culture. In this context it serves as the basis for Teo Kofman's 1986 film of the same title. In the transformation into film, *The Dogs of Night* retained the same sociohistorical meaning as the novel (Medina collaborated with Kofman and Pedro Espinosa on the script), and therefore it is possible to refer to both texts with the same interpretive framework.

In a tradition that extends at least as far back as the Soviet-inspired social realism of the 1930s and 1940s, with the subsequent ideological revisions provided by pro- and anti-Peronist literature of social content in the 1950s, *The Dogs of Night* deals with the pitiful lot of a handful of lumpen drawn from *villas miserias,* slums that surround the periphery of metropolitan Buenos Aires.[1] The film focuses on Mecha and Mingo, the young adult children of a woman who has just died. Like many single women, Mecha and Mingo's mother struggled against extreme poverty to provide a semblance of survival for her children. Unfortunately, Mingo and Mecha do not wholly assimilate her example; the daughter seems to, to some extent, but Mingo has grown up to be a self-centered *machito* (little macho), accustomed to being waited on by his mother and sister and to being a bully outside the home. The greatest effect of their mother's death is the loss of any means of support, and Mecha and Mingo are left to fend for themselves in a hostile world against which their mother can no longer protect them and in which they have learned little in order to survive.

Both the status of Mecha and Mingo and the relationship between them is set up in order to narrate something like a founding text concerning the social world of a pair of innocents who, as in a reinscription of Adam and Eve in the jungle outside the Garden of Eden, must acquire the knowledge for existence within history. When they abandon the shack to seek their fortune in the outside world, they are in a sense shedding a husk that no longer provides them with any protection, since, without their mother there to stave it off, the outside world has already penetrated that threadbare space.

The ways in which the outside world penetrates the shack have principally to do with Mingo's attempts to overcome the dire economic straits in which the two find themselves. *The Dogs of Night* at this point stages a series of narrative actions that are synecdoches of time-honored strategies of economic survival within the social world being portayed. Mecha, like many women of her class and following in the footsteps of her mother, attempts to provide income for the two by accepting odd domestic jobs. Mingo, repeat-

1. Concerning literary themes related to this segment of Argentine social reality, see David William Foster, *Social Realism in Argentine Narrative,* North Carolina Studies in the Romance Languages and Literature (Chapel Hill: University of North Carolina, 1986).

ing the pattern of men of his class, engages in petty thievery. When he is caught and imprisoned, his youthful masculine cockiness is brought up short when he is raped by some of his fellow prisoners, and he leaves prison more bitter than before about his status in society.

Mingo, now with some of the traits of the hardened criminal that prison inevitably provides, sees in the prostitution of his sister the solution to their (his, really) economic difficulties. Mecha has no choice but to accept the prostitution her brother imposes on her, and she is subsequently directly sexually abused by him. As part of his prostitution of Mecha, Mingo decides to seek employment for her as a dance hall "artist." The majority of the novel deals with their wanderings from one small-town cesspool of vice to another. Mecha discovers that the artists are in reality third-rate strippers whose main goal is to attract sexual clients. As she moves through this world, she is befriended by one of the nightclub owners, but when Mingo discovers the relationship developing between the two—a relationship that threatens his control over his sister—he tricks her into leaving for yet another establishment. However, Mecha has had a glimmer of self-reflecting consciousness awakened in her, and in the end she rebels against her brother's exploitation, reacting violently to his aggressive behavior and abandoning him to attempt to make it on her own. Mingo is left adrift in the helplessness of no longer having an object of exploitation with which to defend himself against the world.

Medina, in all of his writings that are set in the context of the socioeconomic realities facing the Argentine urban lumpen, attempts to offer a verisimilar representation of alternatives to total absorption in and annihilation by an oppressive sociohistorical milieu. While in many cases these images are of literal escape— such as the escape from the reformatory in *Las tumbas* (The tombs), released in 1972, or the flight from Mingo in *The Dogs of Night*— only in his most recent writings has Medina begun with resistance and attempted to provide a detailed narrative of alternative social behavior. *El Duke* (1976), which deals with a prizefighter become paramilitary hit man, ends with suicide as the only escape from historical reality; and *Con el trapo en la boca* (With a rag in her mouth), published in 1983, is the flashback of a young woman who has sought a new and liberated self-definition with a lesbian lover after escaping from multiple layers of phallocentric repression by castrating her abusive boyfriend with a straight razor.

The lived experiences of Medina's characters are unrelentingly dreadful, and no euphemistic slippage into the dishonest portrayal of human misery is to be found in these texts. (The morbid, almost voyeuristically pornographic gaze that such unremitting narratives promote belongs to another order of analysis regarding the type of Western reader implied by such fiction in Argentina.) But it is a consequence of the socioculturally valid documentary nature of Medina's rewritings of the social text that the postulation of possibilities for escape or transcendence are especially important. The horizons of a potential rebellion, which might be construed as utopian in strictly sociological terms, become the major feature of literary texts that seek to embody in legitimate elements of the social text signs that, when properly interpreted by the fictional characters, can provide the impulse and the justification for a gesture of alleviating rebellion. Social history is not thereby evaded, is not thereby escaped from; indeed, in a novel like *Con el trapo en la boca* it is only *after* the gesture of repudiation that the first-person narrator is in a position to reconstruct the social text of which she is still a part and in which she definitively installs herself through the self-perpetuating act of telling her own story. The story is, in turn, fossilized as a published narrative, albeit without the verification of realism provided by the genre of Latin American documentary testimonies. *Con el trapo en la boca* remains, in the end, a work of fiction.

Therefore, it is important to stress that the mechanisms providing for the escape from an oppressive lived experience do not derive from something outside social reality, but instead from redemptive elements contained within that reality, which someone, formed within structures of oppression but with the occasion to respond to the potential for escape, is able to perceive and manipulate. After all, this is what Medina himself, formed within the environment described in several of his novels, has been able to do through the medium of fiction; self-reflective narration serves as one means for manipulating the social text so that it can be something other than mechanistically destructive for the individual. In terms of what the contemporary reader is likely to accept as verisimilar, as not mawkish or disingenuous or driven by a hidden agenda divorced from historical reality, the configuration of a possibility for self-determination on the basis of elements present within the social text provides the only basis for a legitimate cultural text.

In *The Dogs of Night* violence, both as a mode of behavior, with all of its ramifications of motivation, response, and structural dynamics, and as one social sign whose meaning only exists within the conjunction of other signs, provides the context for the interpretation of an escape from oppression that is something other than narrative wishful thinking. There are three foci of violence in Medina's novel that are rewritten cinematographically by Kofman. The first focus of violence is the synecdochal microcosm of Argentine society portrayed in the narrative. It is a creatural violence in the sense of deriving from basic circumstances of the human condition: the need for survival in a hostile world, the need to find food and shelter, the need to defend the integrity of one's body against the natural elements and the conflicts of territory provided by contact with other human beings engaged in the same intense struggle in the jungle. The first-person narrator of Jorge Asís's *Los reventados* (Fucked-up individuals), published in 1973, a novel dealing with the pro-Peronist lumpen of the early 1970s, closes with the following assertion: "Matando en la selva, para que no me maten" (Killing in the jungle, so they don't kill me).

The comparison is inescapable between this creatural vision of society, which focuses on Mecha as she fights to keep the household going after her mother's death while Mingo seeks to improve his lot, if only marginally, and the larger, abiding socioeconomic structures of Argentina as they impact proletarian figures like these two young adults. It is not necessary for the film to refer directly to the military government in power in Argentina at the time the novel was published—and banned by that government. This is because it is inevitable that any cultural text of the period (or of the following period of redemocratization, when the film was produced) dealing with socioeconomic conditions will as a matter of course be taken by readers to be pertinent to the circumstances of life under the military. Authoritarian tyranny imposes itself in such all-pervasive ways that it is an authentic point of reference for any cultural production that can, by whatever stretch of the interpretive imagination, evoke it or hold it as an ultimate backdrop for its meaning. And, since the socioeconomic policies of the Proceso were explicitly formulated to produce a concentration of wealth among the few, with the parallel deprivation of resources for the majority, the regime itself provided the horizons for appropriate reading of cultural texts, which is why it had subsequently to ban them: the processes of semiosis vis-à-vis exploitation were all too obvious to the reader. A cultural production like Medina's novel echoed in a symmetrical fashion the policies of the dictatorship and provided by implication a denunciatory analysis of them, and for this reason that production, with its overdetermined resonances as to the effects of those policies, could not be allowed to circulate. Kofman's film, coming during the period in which censorship had been abolished, could take full advantage of these virtually preordained conditions of social meaning.

The violence that *The Dogs of Night* evokes in the context of this originating focus is more than just physical aggression. Certainly, there is plenty of such aggression, made even more vivid in the visual representation of the film. Mingo's macho violence is especially evident, and even more so when it is directed against his sister, specifically when he rapes her. This sequence is constructed around the movement from a general societal violence that we are to understand has been deeply inscribed in Mingo—explicitly, when he is raped in prison, as a function of the prison-as-society equation—to the interpersonal violence of the smallest social nucleus, with the gestures of physical violence being synthesized in one of its most extreme forms, explicit, completed sexual rape. This paradigmatic expression of physical, destructive aggression is complemented—foreshadowed and echoed—by a general climate of danger and fear that is confirmed as justified by recurring patterns of conflict between individuals in the social setting staged by the film.

Verbal insults, acts of discourtesy, passing slights and offenses, refusals to acknowledge the presence of others and to take their needs and demands into account are all part of this recurring pattern of free-floating violence that permeates all spheres of human intercourse and that, in turn, is part of a portrait of a malfunctioning Argentine society. There is no need to attribute this violence to a specific source in the clear terms required of sociological or political discourse, since the parameters of interpretation have al-

ready been overdetermined by the reading horizons within which
the novel and the film circulate. One might well argue that there
are other contexts in which the novel might be read, whether foreign ones that are unaware of all the historical dimensions of Argentina under the military between 1976 and 1983 or Argentine
ones that prefer to see questions of social injustice and the violence it generates as belonging to a social code larger than one
specific set of military governments. The latter position has a certain validity in attempting, if only implicitly, to escape an undue
emphasis on the Proceso as an all-encompassing watershed of the
national experience. Although one could as well insist that the
point of the Proceso is that it is itself only a sign of the larger
sociohistoric process that serves as one constant of the Argentine
experience, and that its only importance lies in its being the most
recent manifestation of that constant, with all of the efficiency deriving from having built on and surpassed previous manifestations.

There is no absolutely persuasive reason to limit the discussion
of an Argentine cultural text by exclusive reference to the nation's
social history, but should one choose to do so, it would not be to
seek substantiating origins but would rather derive from the belief
that cultural texts are, in an original instance, produced against
the immediate background of material history and from the need
to answer a first, not a final, question regarding a primary situation
of experiential meaning. The primary experiential meaning of an
Argentine novel published in 1977 and filmed in 1986 with the
collaboration of the author is principally but not exclusively the
antiphonic relationship between military dictatorship and post-
dictatorship possibilities of revisionism. It is only in this sense that
the primal violence manifested in *The Dogs of Night* is inextrica-
bly linked to a constant of Argentine social history that is rearticu-
lated in the policies of the Proceso and, in turn, reinterpreted by
the novel and film texts at hand. The background of a constant of
social and interpersonal violence does not refer in the final analysis to the military tyranny, but rather the climate of violence sustained and abetted by certain socioeconomic policies *reconfirms*
a historical constant that made the Proceso possible, acceptable,
and defensible as a dynamic constant with Argentine national life.
Only in this way does the context in which Mecha and Mingo
move have an important meaning beyond the trivial story of some

rather arbitrarily personalized exponents of the Argentine urban lumpen proletariat.

When Mecha and Mingo abandon the maternal home, when they move out of the "womb" of protection that has been contaminated by a social reality that their mother, because of her death, can no longer stanch, both are exposed to a cycle of violence that echoes the more restricted violence of the home and confirms the alienation in the world to which the unprotected are routinely subjected. Mecha is the one who most seriously suffers this aggression. In Medina's novel, it comes in the form of the crescendo of humiliations she experiences in the fifth-rate nightclubs where Mingo forces her to perform as a striptease "artiste," with the culmination coming in the form of the pornographic movie she is forced to "star" in and in which she nearly dies. These pages of the novel are perhaps some of the strongest representations in Argentine literature of the trashing of women—or, in more absolute terms, of the trashing of the human body and spirit—and because of the intensity of the portrayal of Mecha's suffering, Medina was accused of morbid voyeurism at the expense of women who are raped.

There is an inescapable bind here (which was also echoed in Zelmar Acevedo's denunciation of homosexual-bashing in *The Tombs*): how to represent with something approximating absolute documentary fidelity the trashing of a woman's body without reproducing, or allowing for the reproduction of, the jubilance some do derive from such behavior. A criterion of documentary fidelity (which literary representation cannot reduplicate because it is, after all, experience displaced by writing) calls for the reproduction of the conditions of abuse itself. The spectator may be either profoundly disgusted or dangerously titillated or, what is even more problematical, caught in a flux between the two emotions. To be caught in such a flux is to reenact the ambivalence of individual responses to what is indelibly inscribed in our social code (in this case, the rape of women and, by extension, the victimization of the weak) and to what our current social teachings wish us to abhor in order to rectify entrenched social history.

Because of the conditions of Argentine cinematography, including the need to appeal to broader audiences than the social vanguard because of financial exigencies, Kofman's film version of

The Dogs of Night suppresses Mecha's starring role in the pornographic movie.[2] What Kofman does retain from the novel is the
graphic portrayal, enhanced by the implacable eye of the camera,
of Mecha's dreadful role as a striptease artiste. Capturing all of the
grimaces and blemishes of her career, the film demonstrates that
the greatest extent to which Mecha is humiliated is in her lack of
awareness of how bad she is and, by extension, in the way in which
she is abused by being obliged to participate in something for which
she has absolutely no talent and, therefore, no potential for success. The culminating scene of this portrayal involves an orgy that,
in the novel, leads to her role in the pornographic film. Kofman
filmed this sequence with enough allegiance to Medina's documentary intent to cause it to be cut from the movie when it was
shown on Argentine national television.

The violence from which Mecha suffers, evidence of which we
see vividly detailed on her body, no matter how much it falls short
of capturing the fuller details of Medina's novel, is, once again, not
just physical. Certainly, she endures enough physical abuse at the
hands of Mingo and the nightclub managers to confirm any feminist version of the rape of women by macho or masculinist society,
and, indeed, these images provided by males (Medina the novelist
and Kofman the director) run the risk of being viewed as voy-
euristic exploitation in themselves. The pornographic movie is a
film within a film that would threaten to subvert the possibilities
as social document of Kofman's cinematographic version by going
beyond the limits of Argentine audience tolerance. Especially with
this segment edited out, the cumulative image of the violence she
suffers is contained in the microscopic accumulation of humiliations in degrading scenes of Mecha as an incompetent actress. The
degree to which she remains unaware of her exploitation becomes,
on the level of the spectator's witness of her performances, an
index of the exponential power of her violent depersonalization.
As much as she is physically abused, she is also spiritually corrupted by Mingo's exploitation of her nonexistent talent and his
repeated if failed attempts to extract from her a measure of artistry.

2. Medina's novel was touching on the allegations that snuff movies were a profitable enterprise made possible by the military's indulgence of its big-money supporters; such movies may have been unique Argentine exports during the period in
which the novel was written.

And in the same degree that she is unaware of this lack of talent, Mecha is exploited by the demands of Mingo and the nightclub managers to render performances of which she is manifestly incapable.

The ironic distance between what the spectator perceives and what Mecha is capable of understanding is the measure of the depersonalizing violence to which she is subjected. As Mecha moves in the larger world beyond her original slum household, from one raunchy striptease theater to another, the experience of violence becomes all the more devastatingly eloquent because the individual who experiences it has come to accept it, to expect it as her lot in life. As Mecha is progressively deadened to the increasing violence to which she is subjected, including threatening advances by the clients of the nightclubs where she appears and sexual abuse by her brother, one perceives a growing insistence on how she is a potent sign for the degradation of the individual made possible by the Argentine social text.

It is only when Mecha is able to break the cycle of her own increasingly thorough humiliations, in the form of the restorative attentions of Ferreyra, one of the nightclub managers, that she is able to aspire toward a perception of the violence against her that the ironic narrative rhetoric has already assured for the reader or spectator. Mecha's revolt against her brother, which closes both the novel and the film, is a ballet of retributive violence in which Mecha, in a concentratedly symbolic fashion, returns to Mingo— himself a sign of a larger sociohistoric dynamic of predatory violence against the individual—all of the physical and emotional aggressions of which she has been the victim throughout their shared story. Kofman rather clumsily handles this closing scene, which is unfortunate. Whereas it might be capricious for one to allege that the two rape scenes lack the final dramatic agony of unsolicited and precipitous corporal penetration, the extended fight between Mecha and Mingo in which she furiously kicks him for having abused her in repeated and multiple ways lacks authenticity—at least, the authenticity that characterizes the documentary criterion of the film as a whole. Were the film to be more symbolic than documentary, the final sequence as an internally coherent symbol would be acceptable. But as a dramatic enactment coextensive with real-life retributive violence, it lacks authenticity, as though real blows to sensitive body parts were not being exchanged or a real interchange of violent fury were not being enacted.

Certainly, such an interchange is what the third focus of violence is all about in *The Dogs of Night,* as a gesture toward the release from automatized and totalized historical violence. There can be no question that Mecha's revolt against Mingo, being essentially a spontaneous outburst of rage and apparently not part of a concerted plan of action, does not in itself constitute a solution. Perhaps it would not be possible to conceive of a solution that would counter violence with violence, whether it be of an injunction to slaves to kill their masters or some other rallying cry. From one point of view, Mecha's fury is nothing more than an extension of the violence Mingo has coordinated against her, the reduplication of the pervasive exploitation to which she has been subjected. Viewed in this fashion, it is not much of a release from that cycle of abuse and might even reinforce it. Seen from another point of view, Mecha's incoherent lashing out against Mingo is cathartic and can lead to more calculated behavior that will point out for her a plan of escape, the first step toward an authentic identity.

The Dogs of Night strategically ends, however, with Mecha's outburst. The film leaves us with the image of Mingo groveling in the face of her fury, and it avoids having to portray the Mecha that will result from this confrontation. The novel is perhaps a bit more categorical. Additionally, the film avoids having to analyze the nature of Mecha's violence within the context of the other foci of violence it echoes and confirms, even if in an oppositional fashion. To be sure, the film enjoys the advantage of adding to Medina's novel the context of the program of redemocratization, whereby the spectator reads the film against the backdrop of the institutional attempts to correct the abuses of military tyranny. But the point to be made here is that *The Dogs of Night* deals not so much with political dictatorship as it does with embedded authoritarian, patriarchal violence that itself makes military tyranny possible. The result is that the connection to be made between redemocratization, which addresses itself to restoring constitutional institutions, and the concreteness of Mecha and Mingo's world does not involve a directly homologous relationship, nor does it address the question of how redemocratization will, or even can, address structural violence of the sort with which Medina's writing as a whole is concerned.[3]

Therefore, Kofman's film is seriously weakened by an inadequate thinking through of Mecha's own violence or, at least, by an inadequate opportunity for the spectator to develop an interpretation of that violence in terms of the semiotic processes of the film. Whereas the free-floating social violence and Mingo's personification of the violence of sexual abuse and exploitation are given ample narrative exposition, Mecha's violence is presented by means of an intense vignette that closes the film, with no larger narrative contextualization to provide conditions for analyzing it in detail. As a consequence, it is left primarily to the spectator to extrapolate a meaning for this gesture. True, all interpretation is a process of extrapolation from the semiotic guidelines provided by the text. But in terms of an expansive narrative exposition, those guidelines provide a certain degree of reiterative pattern that tends to reinforce specific interpretive conclusions. This sort of confirmation is lacking in a concluding vignette that announces a new direction for a text that cannot then be expounded on. In this sense Kofman's ending is not so much inconclusive as it is discontinuous with the way in which the other foci of violence have been handled. If this does not result in confusion, it may result in a measure of frustrating inconclusiveness with regard to Mecha's fate. And

3. An important point, however, lies in the fact that the plight of slum dwellers, whether viewed in socioeconomic terms or in terms of acts that may be interpreted as reflexes of those terms, has not been significantly different under military dictatorships and under democratic governments since 1983. Thus it would be a mistake to imply that political tyranny necessarily makes matters worse or that democracy somehow directly alleviates the living conditions of the economically marginal; this is certainly not the point of Kofman's film. Rather, my point is that structures of violence and exploitation become more transparent, because they are explicitly generalized by official practices, during dictatorships. This does not mean that the latter are more "socially honest" or that democratic governments are necessarily disingenuous in masking the social problems they are unable, or choose not, to remedy. Instead, during dictatorships, violence and exploitation become something like promoted norms, and it is this circumstance that *The Dogs of Night* inquires into. Concerning recent sociological work on the urban poor of Buenos Aires in the context of the redemocratization of Argentine social-science research, consult the essays by Elizabeth Jelin, "Buenos Aires: Class Structure, Public Policy, and the Urban Poor," and Elizabeth Jelin and Pablo Vila, *Podría ser yo: los sectores populares urbanos en imagen y palabra*.

since it is Mecha's fate that the film is primarily concerned with, this is not an inconsequential reservation.

Kofman's movie version of Medina's novel raises some interesting questions about the meaning of culture within the context of Argentine redemocratization in the mid–1980s. One such question is the tendency to oblige the spectator to undertake the not insubstantial extrapolation of the microcosmic details of the film, especially its denouement, from larger issues of the sociopolitical text. That this extrapolation is necessary must be beyond question, since otherwise the film would end up mired in the trivial details of Mecha's debasement, itself a dismally repetitive tale. Since the trivial details of one marginal individual's life must have a larger meaning, especially for the essentially middle-class Argentine filmgoer who is not likely to have much direct contact with people like Mingo and Mecha, it is necessarily in terms of an interpretation of national history, whether the military dictatorships or a larger dynamic of which they are an integral part. The creation of a structural ellipsis between the narratively specific and the historically generic requires a considerable act of interpretation that may well outstrip the competence of all but the most willfully interpretive spectator.

One suspects that a degree of rhetorical modesty takes over at the final point in the film, with Mecha's sudden outburst of violence. Might it not be that the authorial—or auteurial—voice senses the need to shy away from too categorical an endorsement of Mecha's revolt as having larger social meanings? Or is it simply that the spectator must be expected to know what meaning is being mounted here? The issue cannot be decided in favor of one option over the other (short of taking a superficial audience survey—superficial because it can only refer inconclusively to spectator reaction up to the moment of the survey), for the film does not organize interpretive meaning in the final sequence as efficiently as it does up until that point. Whether Mecha's revolt is, like the revolt of democracy against military tyranny, a blind outburst of rage or the seed of an authentic and sustained gesture for reinscribing the individual within history with a constructive personal dignity is a matter as ambiguous as the actual historical moment from which the film garners its primary social meaning. Such symmetry between the cultural text and social history may provide comfort to the spectator anxious that the former not be too jejune in its projections of the latter. Yet at the same time, that symmetry bespeaks a measure of timorous unwillingness of the cultural text to go beyond the documentary chronicle and to provide a meaningfully utopian vision of where we go from here. *The Dogs of Night* comes up short in this fashion, and this limitation is encoded into what I would call the structural imbalance among the three foci of violence in the film; and it will remain for other films to elaborate on the historical projections of what at first might appear to be mere utopian fantasies. This, I will argue, is the sustaining force of Ortiz de Zárate's *Another Love Story,* a film also built around the subject of social violence, but one that also contemplates the effects of its corrective reinscription as an impulse of willful sexual transgression.

▪ ▪ ▪
Kiss of the Spider Woman (*Beso de la mujer araña*): Being Gay and Acting Protocols

1985 must have seemed like the year of the Latin American film. In addition to the immediate enthusiastic response that Puenzo's *The Official Story* received in the United States, his compatriot Héctor Babenco released *Kiss of the Spider Woman;* William Hurt received an Oscar for his leading role as a homosexual imprisoned for, in Latin American legal parlance, "corrupting a minor." Puenzo's films have been produced in part to address an international audience concerning Argentina's dirty war, and *The Official Story* was filmed in Spanish, on location in Argentina, with mostly Argentine actors. By contrast, *Kiss of the Spider Woman,* befitting the greater "Village Voice" reputation of Manuel Puig, the writer on whose novel *El beso de la mujer araña* (1976), Babenco's film is quite faithfully based, was filmed in English, with a leading United States star actor, William Hurt, and a Puerto Rican supporting actor, Raúl Juliá, and on location in Brazil with a number of small-part actors who have appeared repeatedly in Babenco's films. Although Babenco is Argentine by birth and upbringing, his career as a mature director has been in Brazil with films on recognizably Brazilian themes, some of which are also universally Latin

American and Third World, such as the exploitation of children, in his film *Pixote* (1981), which was produced in Portuguese. In the process of recontextualizing the film, the specific references to Argentina in Puig's novel were lost, and the far greater intolerance toward homosexuality in Argentina was transferred to a Brazilian context, where only the most outrageous of sex crimes were likely to be prosecuted, even under the military.

Constitutionally, in neither country is alternative sexual preference or sexual activity between consenting adults considered a crime, although systematic, socially sanctioned discrimination against lesbians and gays routinely takes place in Argentina. Thus, both Puig's novel and Babenco's film turn on the exploitation of the sex offender and the clear message that, rather than being punished for the crime of corrupting a minor, Molina, because of his conviction for a crime that is in itself of scant interest to the police state, is available to be used as a stool pigeon. If he succeeds in extracting information from an imprisoned activist, he has been promised an early release. Numerous critics have pointed out the improbability of such an arrangement, whereby Molina is placed in the same cell as a political prisoner, whose confidence he is supposed to win in order to extract from him the information about his subversive activities the police have been unable to obtain through interrogation under torture. Molina's efforts are successful, to the extent that he gains Arregui's confidence and hears from him about his underground activities. Unfortunately, in the process, Molina falls in love with Arregui, wins a measure of response from the other man (no small feat, given Arregui's dedication to a revolutionary ethos that views homosexuals as self-indulgent decadents who pitifully mimic bourgeois romantic motifs), and promises, when he is released, to contact Arregui's comrades about him. Suspecting they have been double-crossed, the police follow Molina and gun him down as he makes contact with Arregui's comrades, who also fire on Molina in the belief that they, too, have been double-crossed. Arregui, meanwhile, is once again tortured, and if the morphine a sympathetic doctor secretly administers to him is not a lethal dose, the impression is that he does not have long to live in any event.

What has most attracted attention to Puig's novel is the brilliant use of film plots as a counterpoint to the main narrative about

Arregui and Molina. In order to pass the time, and as part of the effort to seduce Arregui, Molina recounts the plots of his favorite movies. In the novel, these movies are a combination of Hollywood staples that might appeal to the stereotypic romantic feminine spectator that such movies both defined and perpetuated and of Nazi propaganda films that the Germans distributed in pro-Axis countries like Argentina and Brazil; by contrast, the novel also includes Jacques Tourneur's cult classic, *The Cat People*. Specifically, the film Molina chooses to entertain Arregui with during the narrative time of the movie is the story of a woman (played by Sônia Braga, involved with the French resistance who dies at the hands of her former comrades when she becomes convinced of the justice of the Hitlerian cause. What is especially clever about the choice of this film is that it serves to provide a reformulation of Molina's views about romantic love and personal sacrifice for the beloved in the form of a highly attractive cultural document like filmic narrative and to offer a statement about political commitment, even if that commitment is here articulated in the terms of the German fascists who are the heroes of the oppressors of both Molina and Arregui.

Because of the special nature of this cultural document, Molina's recounting of the plot and his descriptive embellishments of the visual image provide considerable occasion for metacommentary by Arregui, along with Molina's comments on these comments. Arregui feels himself constrained to point out the noxious fascist ideology underlying the film, to refer to the persecution of homosexuals like Molina in Hitler's Germany, and to refute the concept of romantic-love-until-death that fuels the relations between the film's characters. Molina counters that romantic love constitutes a reason for human beings to care about each other and makes a commitment to political action meaningful because one is then acting in the name of one's beloved. As this dialogue proceeds with its multiple layers of antiphonic commentary, beginning with the controlling juxtaposition of the political plot of the film and the real-life political circumstances of the two men, Arregui seems to move toward accepting Molina's belief in romantic commitment and Molina toward recognizing the validity of Arregui's convictions about political activism. As has been commonly pointed out, while Babenco's film cannot avail itself of materials that are an integral part of Puig's novel, such as the footnotes concerning theories of sexuality, it endorses forthrightly the Marcusian hypothesis that sexual liberation and political liberation are in fact the same process.

Rather than rehearse in detail the evolution of Molina and Arregui's relationship around this proposition, my analysis concerns two sets of complexities and ambiguities in the film. The first set involves the outcome of the ideological exchange between the cell mates, and, as such, it affects the meaning of narrative action. The second involves the acted representation of Molina by William Hurt, which places the film's rhetoric at issue.

It would provide a very neat image of the way in which complex human relations may become resolved to insist that *Kiss of the Spider Woman* ends with a harmonious fusion of the two characters. In such an interpretation, Arregui yields up the macho component of his personality while Molina enlists his ideal of romantic love within a context of the social revolution that will make deep, passionate commitments between individuals fully possible and not just relationships played out within a milieu of repression and persecution. In the Marcusian formulation, any significant manifestation of Eros—not only homosexual—will fall victim to the historical necessity of civilization, which is, after all, one of the universal messages attributed to *Romeo and Juliet*.

In Arregui's case, any modification in his outlook on human relations involves abandoning the homophobic component of traditional Marxist and sixties-style revolutionary activism as much as it involves overcoming the ban on any sort of personal fulfillment such activism imposed. His outlook is demonstrated very vividly in the film when, in a flashback, we see him breaking off with one of his girlfriends because her bourgeois background and the demands she places on him do not jibe with the higher priorities of his clandestine agenda. Presumably, when he acknowledges Molina's expressions of love and offers to make love to him, he accepts both the legitimacy of satisfying personal needs without their having to be dictated as part of a programmatic movement and the legitimacy of Molina's homoerotic desire.

By the same token, Molina's agreement to carry Arregui's message to his comrades and his willingness to double-cross the police should be designed to convince us that an individual who has up until this point acquiesced in seeing himself as nothing more than a screaming queen is now able to understand the demands of revolutionary commitment. In Molina's case this involves risk, not only in double-crossing the police, but also in turning his back on his saintly mother, whose well-being has been his principle reason for existence. Furthermore, Molina seems to understand very well that he is not going to escape with his life, and knowledge of his certain death can be taken as a secure index of his willingness to cooperate with Arregui's cause as the complementary action to the latter's timid but effective expressions of affection toward him. For both, the change of position is momentous because it goes against the rather rigidly defined codes of conduct they have carried with them for a long time, perhaps longer and a bit more diffusely in Molina's case and for a shorter period of time but more intensely stated in Arregui's case. For Molina, it means contaminating his "gay sensibility" with a degree of stern, self-denying seriousness that is anathema to the enjoyment of life, and for Arregui pleasure in Molina's film stories and the real romancing it leads to dilute the single-mindedness that the revolutionary is expected to exhibit. To repeat, it would be ideologically very convenient for the sense of this film if it simply portrayed the commingling in equal portions of the belief systems of the two principal characters.

Yet, Babenco's film is less than clear in showing that this is what in fact takes place. It is not enough to say that such a nicely proportional exchange between two human beings never occurs in real life, since movies, like all cultural documents, are not real life; rather, they are calculated, semiotic creations whose consumer, as part of a process of interpretation of human society, interfaces them with what is believed to be real life. Therefore, it is sufficient that a cultural document insinuate that an interdependency of this sort can take place as something like an ideal of interpersonal relations. However, where *Kiss of the Spider Woman* is ambiguous is not in backing away from or even suggesting an undermining of schematic relations, which might be the case in a document that closes by gesturing toward the abolishment of the closure of meaning it sets up. Instead, it leaves it unclear whether there is any absolute motivation of selflessness in Arregui's and Molina's behaviors. That is, Arregui may well engage in lovemaking with Molina in order to convince him to secretly pass a message to his comrades on the outside, and Molina's agreeing to do so can just as well be motivated by the need to have something to share with the prison authorities in order to win the parole they have dangled in front of him and have threatened to withdraw because he has had so little information to report on Arregui.

Babenco's point in leaving the spectator with this ambiguity cannot really be a gesture of cynicism toward what Molina and Arregui represent as life models, despite the many ways in which the film does reveal details about their personal limitations under the enormous burden, psychological and physical, of imprisonment. Indeed, these limitations are balanced by a host of sacrifices that underscore an intrinsic human nobility in the context of one of society's most degrading institutions. Nor is it reasonable to believe that it is simply directorial ineptitude that subtracts power from the balanced scheme of relations the film seems to have set up from the start, beginning with the contrast between the two characters in physical appearance and behavior. Rather, what seems to be at issue is the interplay between the inner strength and nobility of the individual and the microcosm of power and historical necessity in which these particular individuals are trapped. There can be little doubt that Babenco's film plays on the conventional image of the prison as a synecdoche of the worst of society and, indeed, of the real face of society: the humiliation of the individual through numerous invasions of privacy and continual variations on the violation of the body; the ever-present terror of violence that is actual and impending; the arbitrary exercise of authority both to perpetuate the process of personal debasement and to break down any notions of the legitimate and the just; the shifting ways in which prisoners are at times marginated from society and then made to be participants in the drama of arbitrary power in order to further degrade them and use them as instruments to degrade others, with no opportunity to opt out of the structure.

While *Kiss of the Spider Woman* takes place mostly within the confined space of Molina and Arregui's cell, it is impossible to forget that that cell is part of a larger organism that moves from prison to society in a series of equivalences in which the two men and their personal dilemmas have meaning only because they are part of a previously given social dynamic that they cannot elude. Molina is defined as a queer and then as a criminal before the film begins, and it is only that prior interpretation of him that gives his role any meaning, both in the cultural document we view and in the society it purports to interpret. The same is true for Arregui as regards his earlier definition as a revolutionary guerrilla. In both cases, a history precedes their definition—a history that the film alludes to with some flashbacks and that, not circumstantially, is the background of social history from which they are drawn as exemplars.

What this means is that, although Puig's novel and Babenco's film propose the ideal of a relationship of mutual growth between Molina and Arregui that is underlain by an exchange of commitments between them, their individual stories and the relationship they come to share can never be divorced from the social system that produced the relationship in the first place, giving it its primary controlling meanings. As a consequence of the ways in which Molina and Arregui, their personal stories, and their relationship of ideological exchange exist only because of the larger world of historical necessity in which they live, every aspect of their shared experience is contaminated by the ongoing processes of that larger world. Never able to escape the structure of power in their society, which is reflected in the daily operations of the prison (the interrogation, torture, and food contamination aimed at Arregui; the manipulation of Molina by the warden; and the very fact that they are in a cell together), the two men come to terms with each other within, not outside, the system. If that system is necessarily duplicitous, inescapably corrupting, then their relationship must reflect that fact if it is going to make any sense at all as an interpretation of the social text. Thus, any ambiguity surrounding the motivations of Arregui and Molina can be viewed as deriving, not from their personal inadequacies or from the way in which each decides to use the other to accomplish an important goal, but from the corruption of the system within which they are forced to act.

The hegemony exercised by this system is confirmed by the subsequent failure of the two men to find any fulfillment of their goals: Molina's to get out of prison in order to care for his mother, Arregui's to get a message to his comrades. While one might insist that these goals are replaced by a spiritual or emotional fulfillment centered on the dignifying affection that arises between them, it would take a hopeless romantic to believe that a brief moment of love and anagnorisis justifies the death of the protagonists, whether at the hand of God or as part of the machinations of the spider woman of police power. And it is questionable how much consolation Molina derives from having contacted the guerrillas or how much Arregui obtains from the dream of the spider woman as a figure of Molina and his concept of romantic love. Certainly, both have the right to derive consolation from whatever they can, and it is hardly improper for the film to set the characters up in such a way that their consolations are seen as legitimate. But the social dynamic goes on unchecked, and if the fact that neither man has any meaning for the consciousness of history—it being the only index of the plight of all human beings—is counterbalanced by the new meaning life (no matter how short and ugly) has for each in their relationship of exchange, it must always be borne in mind that all meanings are dictated by the nature of the social text. One might debate how well Babenco brings all of this out without allowing realism about the processes of social history to give way to pessimism about personal nobility. But there is a productive quality in the ambiguity surrounding the conclusion of the film.

An insistence on cultural documents as the locus of the production of semiotic meaning rather than as transparent reflections of an independent reality obliges us to give attention to the role of William Hurt as Molina. Certainly, while there may be Brazilians who look somewhat like Hurt, this actor is necessarily identified immediately by the spectator as a straight North American, retarding from the very outset any "natural" acceptance of him as a Brazilian drag queen. For readers of Puig's novel, each of whom will have formed a mental image of what Molina could have looked like, and for the Latin American spectator in general, seeing Hurt playing the stereotype represented by Molina may have been rather disconcerting; perhaps it even seemed ridiculous. And the fact that Hurt played the part as though imitating Charles Ludlam's female roles in his gay-inspired theater of the ridiculous enhances the initial comicality of Hurt's portrayal, especially since the movie opens with Molina vamping it up outrageously as he begins to spin out his re-creation of the Nazi movie.

Certainly, the major task of the director is to design a film discourse that will engage the sympathy of the spectator for both of the principal characters. There are likely to be any number of viewers who under no circumstances are able to accept a favorable treatment of a gay man or of an urban revolutionary or both. But if there is a choice to be made between the two, Latin American audiences and a broad enough spectrum of North Americans willing to accept revolution in Third World societies even if they have no use for the liberation rhetoric of the sixties will choose to identify quickly enough with Arregui. This identity, in addition to supporting the spectator's views about the struggle against violent repression, will, not unsurprisingly, be largely based on the trim, conventionally manly figure of Raúl Juliá in his representation of Arregui. Arregui talks like a thoughtful man, moves with serious deliberation, and is evidently in as much control of his situation as the circumstances of imprisonment will allow. Moreover, on numerous occasions he utters statements that reflect the ostensibly manly virtues of self-reliance and defiance in the face of any threat of demeanment. Since Juliá plays his part in such an assertively straight fashion, his behavior seems completely natural, which is perhaps why his eventual erotic response to Molina is so particularly riveting; it is out of character with the macho stereotype he embodies. Furthermore, Juliá's macho character matches the romantic notion of the intense guerrilla committed to a cause that excludes all forms of bourgeois conduct, including romantic love and, most especially, any form of sentimental attachment that represents reactionary decadence. In the latter category fall all forms of what is euphemistically called bohemianism, but which specifically includes homosexuality. Although there is a strand of traditional socialism that recognizes the validity of sexual liberation, the dominant ethos inherited by Latin American left-wing revolutionaries, as most vividly demonstrated by the response of the Castro government to Cuban homosexuals, has been the Stalinist belief that homosexuality is a variety of bourgeois decadence, self-indulgence, and one of the all-consuming counterrevolutionary activities that prevent the individual from engaging in sufficiently self-less communitarian action.[4] All of the guerrilla motifs are incarnate in Arregui and in his initial responses to Molina and the cultural manifestations he personifies.

4. Néstor Almendros's 1984 film, *Conducta impropia* (Improper conduct), deals, within the framework of social dissidence in general, with the subject of homosexuals in Cuba and their treatment at the hands of the Castro revolutionaries.

By contrast, Molina, as represented by Hurt, is a stereotypic hysterical queen, flamboyant and preening, dramatic and witty, bitchy and gushing, totally wrapped up in all forms of cultural activities that are ostentatious and artificial (in the root sense of being characterized by artifice). He is fond of extravagant clothes, passionate plots, striking attitudes and poses, and marvelously brilliant details and accessories. On one level, it is difficult not to be enchanted by Hurt's campy, vampy role, difficult not to be captivated by the figure of Molina, who is so determined for the old girl to make the best of it, although this is definitely *not* what she had in mind for a lively party. Hurt-Molina is so outrageous that he is not really threatening to anyone but the most rigid macho, and many spectators will at worst simply agree with Arregui that his cell mate is ridiculously insignificant. Molina as stereotype invites dismissal from the outset.

But what happens is that Molina takes over the film, both because he ends up filling the entire cell with his presence and the accoutrements of his defiant feminine identity, and because of the web of storytelling he weaves and in which Arregui is eventually enmeshed. In the narrated universe that the film is about, Molina becomes the center of any space he occupies, Hurt as an actor takes over the film as cultural artifact, and Babenco ensures that Hurt is at the center of the camera's eye in virtually every scene in which he appears (which is the majority of the film, discounting the segments that belong to the Nazi film Molina renarrates). It is therefore appropriate to ask, from the point of view of cinematographic rhetoric, how effective Hurt's representation of Molina is.

Babenco took a considerable risk by casting Hurt and by allowing (or instructing) him to play the part as a screaming queen. I have already alluded to the problem of Hurt assuming the role of a Brazilian homosexual, which is risky enough, aside from the style in which the part is played. Since Hurt is so obviously *not* a Brazilian (Juliá is not Brazilian either, but he blends with the bit players quite a bit more convincingly), there is already an artificial foregrounding of his role, which is intensified by the fact that Hurt makes no effort to be Brazilian in any way and retains all of the categorically American mannerisms that are part of his actor's persona, such as his twistedly winsome smile. An actor like William

Hurt always plays William Hurt, and there is no exception in *Kiss of the Spider Woman,* except that there is no verisimilitude to be attached to Hurt's identification with the world in which he is here cast.

But of greater significance is the way in which Hurt plays the part of Molina. Certainly there are universal, transcultural modalities associated with sexual identity. If one can refer to culturally nonspecific ways of being macho or of being passively and blushingly feminine, there are also culturally nonspecific elements that make up the identity of the flamboyantly feminine gay male. We can leave aside for the purpose of this discussion the hypothesis that such an urban modality is the result of cross-cultural influences and of the basic homogeneity in Western culture imposed by mass media consumerism. The important point is that Babenco's film has Hurt conforming to one well-established stereotype of the homosexual, and, indeed, among those who adhere to popular homophobic mythologies, to the one defining behavior pattern of the queer. There may be all sorts of things wrong with this conception of homosexuality, and there may be all sorts of dangers— along with reinforcing homophobic attitudes—in such a representation. Puig's novel relies on multiple clichés about the romantic, feminine fairy, and the more demonstrative medium of film renders them especially vividly.

The question is whether this acting protocol enhances or detracts from the character of Molina. On one level, detraction is inevitable for any spectator uncomfortable with the sexual identity Molina represents, and the decision to act the part with no mannerisms associated with the stereotype of the screaming queen would have probably been incalculably confusing for such spectators, who would have been asked to accept the fact that homosexuals may have no uniquely defining mannerisms. This assertion is psychosociologically accurate, but it does not match prevailing popular mythologies about being gay and about being straight, and Juliá plays his role with as much stereotyping of the steely macho as Hurt plays the flamboyant fag. Thus, Hurt's characterization is detracting, or distracting, both because it conforms to homophobic stereotypes and because it is insulting to any consciousness concerning the myriad ways in which the individual combines sexual identity and public persona. The first group is put off by Hurt's Molina because it hates gays, and the second is repulsed by the continued reliance on Peter Lorre or Vincent Price stereotypes (would that Rock Hudson had lived long enough to play a gay, this group might say).

But if one assumes that Babenco and Hurt were taking a calculated risk in order to enhance production of meaning in the film, several possibilities suggest themselves. One is that Molina as played by Hurt must necessarily be appealing because of his reliance on all of the cultural primes associated with nurturing femininity, from his storytelling (which is a way of nurturing the soul of the other) to his concern over Arregui's diet to his nursely ministrations during the latter's bouts of sickness, which Molina knows are the result of the prison authorities' attempts to weaken the prisoner for further interrogation by contaminating his food. Molina is a hovering angel in Arregui's times of distress, and his Crawford-esque invocations of motherhood turn into enough of a real preoccupation over Arregui's welfare, including horror at the devastations wreaked on his body by the authorities, to appeal to most spectators' investment in the maternal imperative.

Too, Hurt conditions his portrayal of the screaming queen by enough sardonic self-reflection to emerge as basically cute and lovable. Hurt's Molina exudes warmth and in this way contradicts the image of the flaming faggot as brash, oblivious to others, and self-involved in the extreme. One of the points that Puig's novel makes, both through narrative framing and through the parallel text embedded in the footnotes in the form of references to documentary treatments on sexuality, is that both Molina and Arregui are playing a part. The difference lies in the fact that our social codes view Arregui's manliness as somehow natural, while Molina's swishiness is unnatural, with accompanying connotations of artificial, perverse, and threatening. *The Kiss of the Spider Woman* intends to show the artificiality of both roles the two men are playing, not in the sense that those roles are illegitimate, but only that both represent the assumption of a given role in the social text. Consequently, the multiple interchange that occurs between the two is not the abandonment of their initial roles, but the amplification of the possible roles they can play in society by acknowledging and assimilating what each had first assumed was the diametrically opposed, mutually excluding persona of the other.

Since Babenco's film cannot rely on the several tiered verbal texts in Puig's novel, including the footnotes, there is less opportunity, without indulging in experimental techniques that reduce general audience appeal, to make use of framing devices to comment extranarratively on the characters' comportment. There would be little to be gained by Juliá becoming somewhat swishy and Hurt suddenly striking macho attitudes, and the real challenge to Hurt is to mediate the essential stereotype from which he departs (evident in the opening frames of the film) by evoking cultural primes like being tender and self-sacrificing that are designed to grab the audience's affection for him. This projection of Molina is carried through to the conclusion of the film, where Hurt, sporting a red scarf and made up for the street, is gunned down by both the police and Arregui's comrades. This is a double blow to his newfound commitment to his former cell mate's cause that is meant to convert him into a tragic figure of dramatic stature.

Hurt is so out of place in this street scene (much of which takes place on the front steps of São Paulo's metropolitan cathedral) that the figure he casts as both Molina and as Hurt the actor is almost ludicrous. But his movement through these final scenes can only serve to remind the spectator that film is not a transparent image of life and social reality, but rather a semiotic artifice that makes use of real-life illusionism in order to propose an interpretation of the social text. The schematism of the Molina-Arregui relationship and the protocols of Hurt's enactment of the Molina character both belong to the province of cinematographic semiosis and not to documentary realism. Spectators who cannot be convinced that Babenco knows the difference and knows how to carry through with his plan for producing filmic meaning will find *Kiss of the Spider Woman* as much disingenuous as they are likely to find it sociohistorically inaccurate.

■ ■ ■

Another Love Story (*Otra historia de amor*): Social Reality and Sexual Utopianism

The cultural policies of the various governments of "national rescue," "national liberation," and the "process of national reorganization" are so draconian and bring with them so many mechanisms of direct oppression and wide-ranging repression (the worst of which is self-censorship, which may often be unconscious, in order to avoid problems) that there tends to be an enormous cultural resurgence when institutional democracy is restored. Unfortunately, such restorations tend to be transitory, with any resurgence providing yet another basis for a renewed round of the persecution of the "subversive," "the pornographic," "the anti-X." The "X" might stand for whatever cluster of right-wing idealized institutions are being considered threatened at the moment by culture: Catholic tradition, the family, the armed forces, sexual difference, and, the most idealized of all, nationhood itself. But the cultural resurgences in Argentina following the first Peronist period in the late fifties and early sixties, briefly following the military dictatorships between 1966 and 1973, and during the program of redemocratization in the early 1980s following the Proceso are impressive. Logically enough, a significant ingredient of each resurgence is the manifestation of those cultural modalities or themes that were precisely the object of control by superseded dictatorial regimes.

One such manifestation is the whole complex of erotic love. Love and sex have been so problematical for nationalist military regimes in Argentina that, except in their most Disneyish or Romeo-and-Juliet demonstrations, they usually suffer the rigors of censorship. Perhaps the only exception would be a cultural text that portrays, in the spirit of a movie like *Fatal Attraction,* the hellfire consequences of any deviation from narrowly defined concepts of moral rectitude where love and the expression of sexuality are concerned. The erotic and the sexual as categories of thought and behavior in and of themselves are not even to be contemplated.

In the case of Américo Ortiz de Zárate's *Another Love Story* (1986), the function of the prenominal *another* brings out this interplay between a period of cultural muteness, in which a legitimate voice is denied to a sociopolitical phenomenon, and a subsequent period of cultural production in which it is allowed to speak its name. On the one hand, "another story" refers to a continuum of cultural documents wherein love as a legitimate object of sustained analysis, as opposed to mythification, is underscored. Yet, in reality, another, yet one more, story of love is part of a restoration of the ability to talk about such a complex human phenomenon in such a dangerously influential medium as the film, which, because it is considered to be so dangerously influential, is one of the first cultural realms from which love is banned by censorship.

But on the other hand, Ortiz de Zárate's film leads us to construe the meaning of the prenominal in another fashion. Here "other" refers to the Other in a very real sense, because the story of love being added to the continuum is homoerotic in nature. What is being added to the inventory of filmic romance tales is one of the realities of love aggressively eliminated by programs of cultural disarticulation. As a consequence, a period of recovery and resurgence such as the one that took place in Argentina as part of the official program of redemocratization must necessarily involve expanding the registry of legitimate thematic representations. What is in fact taking place is the amplification of the realm of cultural production so that it may attain a reasonable homology with the realm of social reality. Whereas one could expect there to be a coincidence between the "culturemes" of social reality and their rewriting as themes in an honest practice of cultural production, it is the goal of censorship to purge whole segments of cultural production and to implement in their place practices with no legitimate anchoring in social reality (that is, so-called escapist, evasionist, or "mystificational" culture). Homosexuality is clearly one of the segments of social reality that repressive cultural programs (among others, of course) that are founded on fascist, nationalistic principles consider demonic, and pastel-colored notions of romantic love are considered to be its negative valence. Both topics are involved in Ortiz de Zárate's attempt to deal with a homosexual love affair.

The "coming out" of Y (the protagonists of the film are never named) in terms of a newly discovered sexuality is necessarily coextensive with the expression of personal identity permitted by taking seriously individual freedoms in a redemocratized Argentina. (Indeed, the very possibility that Ortiz de Zárate's movie and a few others like it could even be made in the first place is the result of an embrace of individual freedom.) As a consequence, Y moves between two worlds that have a meaning larger than merely that of personal sexual preference. Following the byword that "the personal is political," the structure of the decision that Y takes on the basis of the affair that emerges with Z is fundamentally a political affirmation. It is a political affirmation not just because the ability to make that decision and to abide by it, with all the attendant complications it will bring, is conditioned by political circumstances; it is the reaffirmation of the privacy of the body as guaranteed by the Argentine constitution and the suspension of the reactionary moral crusade of the dictatorship.

It is even more so a political affirmation because, beyond active social and political institutions like the church, the military, and the government—the macrostructural elements of Argentine society—on the microstructural level of nuclear human relations, individual behavior both embodies and constitutes the parameters of the macrostructure. It is not necessary here to review the extensive body of theoretical writings concerning the interaction between personal horizons of the sociopolitical and institutionalized dynamics; this is essentially the principal constitutive force of human society. But in terms of fictional cultural texts about actual people, especially when they are portrayed against a backdrop of the sociohistoric that, in the case of Argentina, is never far removed and is even less so in the mid–1980s, the lives of those people can only be read as enacting the social macrostructure. Moreover, the widely promulgated conventions of contemporary feminism, gay liberation, and ethnic identity serve to ensure that the personal is given a principally political reading.

Thus, *Another Love Story* moves in two narrative spaces corresponding to two radically disjunctive social matrixes. The first space is the sober and repeatedly conflictual world of Y's thoroughly middle-class marriage. There is nothing specifically wrong with this marriage, other than stock criticisms regarding trite or staid or dehumanizing values associated with a bourgeoisie always fearful of losing its dignity and, underlying it all, its place in society. Y's life in this context is satisfactory in many ways, and he enjoys the prerogatives of a successful middle-level manager in a commercial concern, including the macho's time-honored ability to pay for extramarital sexual escapades. He is handsome, dresses well, is well respected, and enjoys all of the comforts promised to him for success and conformity by the Argentine advertising media.

When Y discovers himself suddenly to be the object of Z's aggressive attentions, the neat patterns of his world are altered. Z superficially fulfills the image of the Argentine swinging playboy;

in addition to having handsome, smiling looks, he engages people's sympathy via a form of stereotypic roguish behavior. The only significant difference is that his sexual preference is homosexual; the individual on whom he puts a series of clever moves, drawn from the arsenal of the successful playboy, is Y. Part of the narrative complication of the film, of course, is that Y does not know how to react. At first confused, then rather intrigued, he pursues a number of acts designed to underscore for the viewer the fact that he is moving in totally alien territory. When he subsequently accepts Z's advances, the unknown becomes the way in which he must deal with his family, particularly since, through an act of petty revenge, one of his co-workers (a woman) informs his wife about the new sort of sexual adventurism in which he is involved. As a clear articulation of the relationship between the personal and the political, Y is rejected by his wife, who attempts to commit suicide and, in general, echoes behavior in a paradigmatic soap-opera script; and he is essentially repudiated by his teenage son, completely lacking in any knowledge as to how to cope with the new development in his father's life. Indeed, this is one of the most critical aspects of the film: the lack of a public discourse on homosexuality in Argentina means that Y's son has absolutely no social points of reference for dealing now with his father—no points of reference beyond the unreflectively homophobic, which is not of much use in the case of a relationship that has been so far defined by respect.

It is possible to view the disjunctive narrative spaces of the film as the before and after of Y's family life, the series of antiphonic relationships that are defined by reactions to conformity that has been replaced by scandalous sexual outlawry (at least in a conventional if not a strictly legal sense of the word). Yet, in reality, little attention is paid to the somber tones of Y's rejection by his family. Indeed, the drastic act of his wife, who will now file for formal separation, and the alienation of his son force Y to separate himself from the heterosexual family unit in a way he might not have really preferred to do. The encouragement of his good-natured and sympathetic aunt, who understands her nephew's need to do something else with his life, is, therefore, especially important for his acceptance of the need to abandon a domestic arrangement that no longer holds a life for him.

The alternate space, the sustained other pole of Y's existence becomes his erotic relationship with Z. Availing himself of the liberties of his masculinist world, Y is able to set up a love nest for himself and Z, which would have worked fine as long as his wife had not been informed about its existence by the disgruntled coworker. From Y's point of view, no doubt, a complementary relationship exists between two different objects of sexual passion. It is Y's wife's discovery that actually creates conflict, as it would appear that Z is not driven to assert exclusive domain over Y. Z does, however, seem in fact to achieve this at the end of the film. Y, offered a good position in Spain, at the last moment misses his plane to return to Z's arms, providing *Another Love Story* with a conventional happy ending that is nevertheless satisfying in the unostentatious way in which it is offered as a verisimilar denouement to the narrative scheme enunciated up to that point.

What does happen in the course of this resolution is the confrontation between two erotic spaces, with a movement from the primacy of one, to the conflict between them, and then to the ascendancy of the second. It is important to understand that this movement does not rest on the rejection of heterosexuality as illegitimate, either because it is hypocritical or because it is castrating of human passion. Such a radical gay separatism might be ideologically defensible, although it is doubtful if it would find much support among anything other than a very select movie audience. The simple fact is that Ortiz de Zárate is very discreet in his handling of homosexuality, both in its conflicts with dominant heterosexism and, in cinematographic terms, in its details as a form of erotic passion. It is the homophobia within heterosexism, viewed in the various melodramatic reactions to Y and Z, that makes the two realms I have described disjunctive, and not any impulse of radical gay separatism on the part of the characters or the director. One might argue, though, that the inclusion in the film of melodramatic homophobia is an oblique way of predisposing the spectator toward an unstated separatism that is quite implied by the final sequence of the events, especially with Y's turning away from a very attractive job offer in a place where Z cannot accompany him.

One of the keys to Ortiz de Zárate's legitimation of homosexuality in nonradical terms lies with the title of his movie. The conjunction of terms *otra historia* allows several readings. In one sense, it is "just" one more love story that confirms melodramatic narrative conventions: the other lover, the breakup, the realignments, all attended by high-pitched emotional discharges. Like the famous gay play by Bill Solly and Donald Ward, *Boy Meets Boy: A Musical Comedy in Two Acts* (1975), wherein homosexual pairing is treated as a thoroughly naturalized matter of sentimental liaisons within the paradigm of popular-culture boy-meets-girl formulas, Ortiz de Zárate's film handles the Y and Z love affair as confirming an age-old rite of passage in human events: the objects of people's passion change, and life goes on after the usual course of readjustments. Melodramatic trappings only serve to underscore the movement, and instead of deterring it, they give it a sense of finality, or at least restored equilibrium, when the attendant emotional discharges have taken place, whether these are experienced directly by the participants or vicariously by the spectators, who are encoded into the circuit of responses by the nature of melodramatic rhetoric.

Another way of reading the film's title is not as another story, but as a story that happens to be about love. That is, *otra* is placed in opposition to the unitary meaning of *historia de amor,* with all of the heterosexist overtones that that phrase possesses. Love stories, as they have been monumentalized in Western culture—first, with love as an ideological construct, and then in the form of narrative morphologies about love—must, by virtue of the ideological definition of love, involve a man and a woman as fully formed and fully differentiated gender categories. Homogeneric characters in these narratives cannot be involved in a love relationship; what they possess may be erotic passion and it will probably be viewed as destructive because eros is ideologically inscribed as antithetical to romantic love, but it will certainly not be viewed as love, by virtue of inappropriate role fulfillment. The semantic structure of romantic love has no room for homosexuality or, indeed, any form of nonheterosexual love. Since romantic love customarily finds its culmination in the production of babies, there are even many forms of heterosexual love that are routinely excluded, which is, after all, one of the points of the geriatric passion of characters in Gabriel García Márquez's *El amor en los tiempos del cólera* (Love in the time of cholera), published in 1985. Like Griselda Gambaro's trenchant neo-Frankenstein play, with its ironic title, *Nada que ver con otra historia* (Nothing to do with another story), produced in

1972, Ortiz de Zárate's movie is very much an *other,* rather than *another,* love story when viewed against standard texts that establish the motifs of Western romantic love. The fact that so many of our movies turn on these motifs truly makes the relationship between Y and Z an *other* story, a story of the other. Moreover, Argentina may not have the legal constraints against manifestations of homoeroticism that continue to exist in large segments of the United States, but one can be assured that homophobia is even less checked in that country than in the United States by any sense of indulgence toward alternate life-styles. Gay bashing is perhaps not the order of the day in Argentina (although acts of violence do occur in contexts wherever machismo predominates), but gays do constitute a shadow society in a country whose daily social practices rest so firmly on the constraints of middle-class respectability.

And there is even a third sense in which Ortiz de Zárate's title suggests the narration of another love story. It has been amply documented that up until the revisionary gay liberation, the dominant fashion in which homosexual representations have entered Western culture has been in terms of the tragic mode, with its shading off into the melodramatic. Some instances of the comic may be pointed to, but they involve a satiric thrust directed against gays and not against the preposterous social codes that find them ridiculous or outrageous. Notions concerning the "problem of homosexuality" have allowed for the explication of the tragic consequences deriving either from the crime against nature—Oscar Wilde's Dorian Gray made over into an omnivorously corrupting homoerotic monster—or from the lack of adequate understanding and treatment of an instance of psychosexual weakness to be found in some individuals, such as the misunderstood, and consequently suicidal, effeminate waif, who may fall victim to the hardened Dorian Grays. Whereas one cannot deny the anguish that is likely to derive from a nondominant sexual orientation, which is homologous with the conflicts that may stem from a minority religious or political orientation, the perception that it is possible to be gay and not to have either to commit suicide or to submit to aggressive humiliations, including therapy and shock treatments, because of it must count as an important revisionist stage of a contemporary liberationist sexual discourse. (One will leave aside for the purposes of this discussion the dangers inherent in a discourse that imposes a Pollyanna-like attitude toward untroubled free sex.)

Where *Another Love Story* interfaces with this discourse is in
rejecting the portrayal of homosexuality as a tragic mode of existence. Y and Z may have a lot of problems in their relationship, but
the attitude is, What relationship doesn't? Therefore, Y and Z are
able to face the demands of their love without the film having to
bring concepts of sex and love into a thunderous harmony that
would sweep all objections before it and without their having to
serve as tragic figures in a plot whose denouement would be ca-
thartically pedagogical. Indeed, the ending of the film plays with
the motif of loss that is inherent to the tragic mode, since alienation, mutilation, and death are all extreme varieties of the loss of
the object of desire. Just when it looks as though Z will lose Y
because of the superb job offer in Spain, a loss that would be inevitable in "higher" moral terms because the real business of life must
go on, the inner logic of their commitment to each other asserts
itself with such a rhetoric of naturalness that one could even be led
to believe that Y had no intention of leaving Z in the first place and
that the whole process of departure for Ezeiza was nothing more
than a big practical joke. This may be stretching a point, but the
simple fact of the narrative action is that the union of Y and Z is
reasserted at the end of the film as entirely consonant with the
circumstances that their lives have now assumed. Not that there
will be no problems—no one believes that even the silliest of happy-
ending closures to cultural texts mean that the quotidian stresses
of life have been abolished—but the conflicts will not derive from
the intrinsic illegitimacy of the relationship that is the defining
narrative matrix. Thus, *Another Love Story* is involved essentially
in legitimating a certain kind of story referring to human passion,
one in which mutually satisfactory homosexual love is played out,
is an *other* register of love that is, if not ahistorically happy, nevertheless legitimate.

Of considerable interest are the ways in which Ortiz de Zárate
goes about legitimating Y and Z's love affair as part of the overrid-
ing need for a costly production not to alienate the paying audience that will permit its circulation.[5] Unlike the print media, commercial films must still not be audacious. This is especially so in
Argentina, where norms of public decency are more clearly de-

---

5. The director's problems in raising the money to make this film have assumed
almost legendary dimensions, enhanced by his death in 1989 from AIDS.

fined and enforced than in western Europe and even the United States, where the "hot" medium of the film makes it more suspect than books and magazines, where film is still almost a luxury item (in terms of the local economy, movie tickets in Argentina cost approximately three times what they do in the U.S.), and where, when all is said and done, Argentine audiences will always prefer the most ideologically disingenuous American movie to a "serious" national film. Thus a director like Ortiz de Zárate has a very tough task: how to deal with a subject circumscribed by general social condemnation while at the same time not alienating a presumed public made up in large part of those who are predisposed to condemn the film. Certainly, the film could have been aimed at the already converted, but that would have limited its commercial possibilities and, perhaps more than anything else, undermined the liberalizing program of Argentine cultural production within whose parameters *Another Love Story,* on the heels of the homophobic military tyranny, was planned.

Let me enumerate some details about Y and Z and their presence in the film that confirm what I have been so far implying and now wish to state categorically: that Ortiz de Zárate had really no other choice than to make his gay lovers "decent" gay lovers within the confines of the Argentine social code. As such, they and their relationship preclude any meaningful critical reflections on the bedrock conditions of eroticism in Argentine society. Both men belong to the broad Argentine middle class; both are businessmen who look, dress, and conduct themselves accordingly. Moreover, in the best tradition of Hollywood-type films, both are physically fit and attractive, and it is only the director's reserve that keeps us from seeing, as we now can so confidently expect to see as Hollywood assimilates the latest trends, well-sculpted buttocks and symmetrically tufted armpits and navels.[6] Y is an attentive and responsible enough family man, and Z cares for his ailing mother, which is why he cannot accompany Y to Spain. Both are respectful toward their co-workers: Y is serious and reserved, and Z displays the roguish style that seems to be so endearing to a certain

6. Fashion-model types of male derrieres and genitals have begun to appear in Argentine films. For example, one gets a glimpse of Hugo Soto's rear in *Man Facing Southeast,* and *Gracias por el fuego* (Thanks for the light), released in 1984, contains frontal nudity.

Argentine public sector. Y and Z are in all respects mature and balanced, so much so that one can see their homosexuality—Z's overtly declared preference and Y's emerging one—either as the only thing "wrong" with them or as quite simply a natural extension of their well-tuned equilibrium. The ideological gesture of *Another Love Story* is reasonably directed toward the latter, since the whole narrative elaboration of the film is built around confirming the internal coherence of their life decision as a "natural" extension of their human nature.

In terms of narrative representation, the details of homoerotic passion are so discreet that the embarrassed moviegoer has little specifically to object to, while the imaginative spectator might well wonder if Y and Z really have any idea of what all they are supposed to be doing to make it worth the conflicts they are going to have to face. There is only the faintest suggestion of corporal unveiling, the barest glimmer of passionate embrace, only the slightest hint at the multiple complexities of mingling of bodies and minds in ways that confirm the great importance attached to the erotic, especially in anything that can be called its transgressive dimensions. Earnest sex as a real fact of life is absent from this film, and the ways in which Y and Z come together are virtually a parody of the metonymical minimalism of Nō theatrics. The most "advanced" depiction of sex is in a shared bathtub scene, but the culminating touch between the two men is filmed through the blurred refraction of the wine bottle meant to signal the celebratory nature of their union. This touch of kitsch may be meant to give the scene some artistic class, though it may also mean the filmmaker lost his nerve. Perhaps there is a secondary track of meaning that is a parody of the conventions of heterosexual love scenes in the high romantic mode. In any case, the film becomes wrenchingly self-parodic in a postmodernist way that has nothing to do with its overall earnestness as a text revindicating basic human decencies. In the final analysis, once Y's wife and son have been tucked conveniently away in the realm of fossilized moral codes, everyone keeps smiling in *Another Love Story* as though the general level of elation were sufficient to sweep the most skeptical spectator into enthusiastic endorsement of a natural homoerotic passion assimilable within the discourse of dominant heterosexual love, romantic or otherwise.

Although romantic love may retain its sentimental hold on general Argentine feelings, there is a rich vein of cultural production, both elitist and popular, that is able to recognize more rough-edged material manifestations of the erotic than greeting-card romance. A survey of such manifestations would necessarily begin with the tango, a music, dance, and poetry phenomenon whose stark harshness in various registers, starting with the inverse sentimentality of its glamorization of emotional sadomasochism, has become enough of an integral part of Argentine culture to anchor multiple varieties of nonromantic love. Mass-circulation writers like Enrique Medina have charted the many aspects of nonromantic sexual passion and have raised a host of ideological problems that cannot be gone into here, the first of which is the antifeminist voyeurism Medina has often been accused of. And a richly modernist writer like Julio Cortázar has proffered all sorts of suggestions about an antiromantic interpretation of sex, though he, too, is not without readers troubled by the imbalances his fiction reveals in the process of addressing the erotic.

What happens in Ortiz de Zárate's film, however, is that in the process of proposing a well-scrubbed legitimacy and naturalness for homoerotic passion, the dirty work of sex is left behind. I do not by this mean to say that the film is deficient for eschewing the depiction of warts-and-all sexual hydraulics, but only that it overlooks the fact that sex, like all of life, is mired in the slime of history. One way of signaling the fact that the narrative text is focusing on the material nature of history is to refer now and then to what really happens, which in the case of sex means some real, unmistakable sexual intercourse. The point of portraying unmistakable acts in contemporary culture is to remedy the antimaterialistic condition of our prevailing interpretations of sex and to remind us that whatever romantic love, as an ideology to be decried, means, it first and foremost means subtracting the dirtiness from sex. Alternatively, the narrative can allegorize or render as metonymy the dirtiness of life by portraying the implications of the material, which is usually what dirty jokes do. I don't think there is a single torrid sex scene in all of Faulkner's fiction, but the harsh realities of sex get communicated just the same, and this is true of the very best of the great Hollywood movies circumscribed by the Hayes Act.

For the immediate sociohistorical purposes of Ortiz de Zárate's film, however, the synecdochal representation of the material conditions of sex is what is most lacking. Aside from the sequences relating to the melodramatic reactions of Y's family to his sexual realignment, aside from the echoes this is meant to have vis-à-vis the bourgeois hypocrisies regarding sex in Argentina, there is little else in the way of allusion to the social dynamics of sex in that society. True, there is the matter of the revenge one of the office workers takes against Y by sending an anonymous denunciation to his wife; that this is a productive and almost socially acceptable form of conduct is one manifestation of a reigning hypocrisy. Then there are the problems that the two men have with the directors of the company for which they work, since their superiors cannot accept the possible effects that scandal may have on their operations. This conflict between the realities of business and human dignity, nevertheless, gets localized in the film in terms of the meanness of one set of employers, and there is no hint of the coextensive relations between business, morals, and authoritarian tyranny that gets raised in the figure of Roberto in Puenzo's *The Official Story*. Y and Z end up persecuted by their employers for their personal sexual lives. But that persecution assumes no truly threatening dimensions, since Y, at least, has resources, including a subsequent job offer outside the country, to sustain them both economically (too, there is no mention of the consequences to him of Argentina's rather draconian separation settlements). And no attempt is made to link the attitudes of their employers to larger questions of political ideologies regarding sexual transgression in Argentina, such as one finds with respect to the United States in Harvey Fierstein's movie version of *The Torch Song Trilogy*.

Put in rather simplistic terms, but terms that bespeak this viewer's dissatisfaction over the absence of real-life harsh edges in Ortiz de Zárate's film, Y and Z get off too easily. Again, it is a matter of balance. In the desire to show that homosexual love need be neither melodramatic—or, at least, any more melodramatic than life generally is—nor tragic, *Another Love Story* gives the impression that there are no tragic consequences to flow from transgressive sexual practices. But, of course, there are. It does not require the image of a blowtorch to the genitals, as in Tennessee Williams's veiled homosexual fugue, *Orpheus Descending*, or castration, as in several of Faulkner's novels. But gays are bashed in real life, and the real life of Argentina under the military involved a lot more than just the symbolic humiliations of long-haired youth, as the attractive recruits who pulled the men's room entrapment detail could well attest. If Western bourgeois sexual morality in general exercises a chilling effect on the erotic manipulation of the body, with varied bloody consequences for the too overt manifestation of it, the double transgressiveness of homosexuality merits aggressions of a higher exponential order. Y and Z get off very lightly for their transgressions, and even Y's wife's suicide attempt serves to trivialize her suffering because she translates it into a conventional melodramatic response, thereby depriving the spectator of the need to understand that she, too, is a victim of sexual hypocrisy and not just a convenient and then expendable sign for it.

In interpreting the possibilities of homosexual love that is salutarily neither melodramatic nor tragic, Ortiz de Zárate expunges anything other than the most fleeting references to the historically material and dirty, the not easily allayed anguishes, the truly bloody aggressions, the often disastrous misunderstandings occasioned by duplicitous and defective social codes—in short, the real passion of sex when it is a transgressively erotic manipulation of the body with deeply resonant sociopolitical consequences. In the desire to make homosexuality palatable, or at least nonthreatening, to a general Argentine movie audience, Ortiz de Zárate has bleached out of his narrative fabric any solid understanding of how homosexuality remains, whether one wants it to or not, a threatening experience for the individual circumscribed by the sociopolitical code in Argentina. And the code cannot be transcended, any more than history can ever in any way be stepped out of, merely by good intentions. Over and over again, the deceptive realism of film hides the fact that the text is overlooking significant, implacably present, sectors of reality in order to install a preferred social meaning. That meaning may, indeed, be preferable, beginning with the most modest definitions of human dignity; but what is an implacable hindrance to its realization cannot simply be written out of the social text by ignoring it in the interpretive revisions of the text. By uncovering and representing aspects of social reality ignored by the Argentine cultural tradition, a movie like *Another Love Story* may give the impression that it has said what needs to be said, when, in fact, significant silences still remain to be spoken. *Another Love Story* is a good film, and it speaks a revisionist message that is salutary, but in doing so with such good cheer, it dodges around several hurdles of Argentine sociopolitical reality that are there, whether the film wants them to be or not. And the fact that this movie never really had the impact that any movie interpreting sexual practices ought to have is one reflex of the existence of those hurdles.

CONCLUSION

Perhaps it would be exaggerated speculation to assert that film is the most representative manifestation of the culture of Argentine redemocratization. Film is a highly visible commercial product and one that can now be safely, although not exclusively, inscribed within the orbit of high or elite culture. As such, it ought not distract attention from the truly heterogeneous display of popular culture processes that have emerged since censorship was lifted and the market demand took hold for a multiplicity of products that could in no way have been possible under the dictatorship: rock music and songs appealing to diverse sectors of Argentina's extensive youth culture; television programming with both a national and international focus; magazines of all types, especially humor and satirical publications; mass spectacles, including concerts and broad-audience reviews; paraphernalia, such as bumper stickers, buttons, t-shirts, and posters, that proclaim previously proscribed feelings or identities, even those relating to sex. In the face of this wealth of cultural production, one would be well advised not to inflate the importance of genres that, while they may be of interest because of the concentrated originality of creative effort underlying them, may perhaps have not had the general societal impact enjoyed by mass consumer products.

Despite an unfavorable economic situation that has even worsened under democracy since the artificial supports of the tyranny were removed, redemocratization unleashed in the early 1980s, in an Argentina always ready to consume enthusiastically the latest cultural fashions, an intense desire to assimilate products that the dictatorship had suppressed. As I have argued from the outset of this study, the appeal of the filmmaking during the period of redemocratization turned out to be severely circumscribed by the greater priority of audiences to see the many foreign films that had either been banned by the junta's censors or shown in cut versions.

Yet when one examines the privileged position of filmmaking vis-à-vis other high culture genres during the period in question, there is an undeniable basis for viewing it as exceptionally significant. Theater made its greatest contribution in the form of Teatro Abierto, which between 1981 and 1983 defied in dramatic terms (double entendre intended) the structures of repression. Although some denunciatory works of fiction, such as those by Marta Lynch, Jorge Asís, and Enrique Medina, did circulate during the tyranny, it was probably the most visible form of Argentine culture in exile, in both Spanish and in translation, as witnessed by the works of David Viñas, Manuel Puig, Griselda Gambaro. Poetry always has a select appeal, although the poet Alejandra Pizarnik, who committed suicide in 1972, emerged as something of a cult figure. Her *La condesa sangrienta* (The bloody countess), on the sadistic exploits of the seventeenth-century lesbian Hungarian countess Erzébet Báthory, was reissued in 1976 and understandably read as a metaphor of human rights abuses.[1] And the sociopolitical essay, which enjoyed some prominence during the transition between the periods of the military and of constitutional democracy, can be viewed as a more focused derivative of the many voices of oppositional journalism that found channels of expression during the military period, especially since most of the authors of book-length exposés after 1983 were professional journalists.[2]

Filmmaking since 1983 is essentially coterminous with the process of redemocratization. Thus, all of the films examined herein bear directly on questions of sociopolitical dissent, whether understood in terms of explicit public acts or interpreted under the aegis of the slogan "the private is political," which suggests the way in which ideological interpretations are drawn from a consideration of the erotic and the sexual. Even those films that, on the one hand, deal with intensely intimate questions (like *Another Love Story*) or, on the other, deal with superficially local-color

1. David William Foster, "Fiction and the Sociopolitical Text: Violence, the Body, and Cultural Responses in Argentine Literature in the Context of Military Tyranny."

2. David William Foster, "Argentine Sociopolitical Commentary, the Malvinas Conflict, and Beyond: Rhetoricizing a National Experience."

issues (like *South Side*) can only with great effort not be read as dealing with larger, unresolved tensions in Argentine society, despite the much vaunted return to institutional democracy. Certainly, the return to democracy provided the opportunity to deal with these questions. And cultural products like the film were inevitably going to invite the spectator to view them as examining critically precisely those topics that the constitutional government had been unable to address satisfactorily. And, to the extent that Argentina viewed itself as modeling for other Latin American countries emerging from a decade or more of military tyranny the possibilities of a thoroughly redemocratized society, a highly international cultural phenomenon like the film lent itself eloquently to a process of interpretation leading from the immediately personal or the immediately local to larger and abiding questions of Latin American society. Those questions concerned individuals' legitimate control of their own bodies, the opportunities to question established authority and to unmask its disingenuous strategies for self-perpetuation, and the structures whereby sociopolitical repression remains unchanged despite manifest revisionary attitudes. In this sense, the despair of the psychiatrist at the end of *Man Facing Southeast* enunciates all of the concern these films sought to activate over the true process of social—and, therefore, personal—reorganization that remains yet to be enacted.

Films that were produced in Argentina before 1983 and under the shadow of the junta were in the main commercial ventures with inconsequential or nonexistent artistic dimensions. Or, at any rate, the films that were made with artistic pretensions could hardly have anything to do with the facts of military rule, for example, Mario Sabato's 1979 *El poder de las tinieblas* (The power of darkness), based on the novel *Sobre héroes y tumbas* (On heroes and tombs) by his father, Ernesto Sabato. As Peter B. Schumann has written:

> The consequences [of the military dictatorship] were disastrous for Argentine cinematography. A great many filmmakers saw themselves forced to go abroad to escape the death threats: Gerardo Vallejo and Lautaro Murúa, who only by chance survived the bombs that exploded in their homes; Octavio Getino and Fernando Solanas, Humberto Ríos and Rodolfo Kuhn, Mauricio Beru and Jorge Cedrón, and including, although only for a short time, Leopoldo Torre Nilson, along with

many others, the majority of the most well known figures. Some were kidnapped and probably killed, as occurred with Raymundo Gleyzer and Pablo Szir; likewise with the authors and scriptwriters Haroldo Conti and Rodolfo Walsh. Others, like Enrique Juárez, were executed.

The exodus, the repression, the prohibitions on exercising the profession, and the censorship undermined the substance of Argentine cinematography. The amount of films released dropped from 35 in 1975 to 16 in 1976, to again rise to 32 in 1979 and, finally, reached its lowest point in 1982 with only 17 full feature films; all this as a consequence of the disastrous political economy, of the lack of state incentives, and of the problems stemming from censorship.[3]

The fact that redemocratization meant that by late 1983 films could be made without the restrictions of censorship or the threats of violence against those involved and the fact that the Alfonsín government was willing to provide subsidies provided a confluence of circumstances affording film as a cultural genre a clearly defined fresh beginning. And the steady economic decline that occurred throughout the Alfonsín period and on into the presidency of Carlos Menem, which began in 1989, translated into the cessation of government subsidies, which itself translated into the effective demise of an independent cinematography driven primarily by creative considerations. The need to turn a profit may not necessarily imply artistic or ideological compromises, but within the overall precarious panorama of Latin American film production it cannot be considered a stimulus either. To judge by the uneven quality of María Luisa Bemberg's 1990 film on Sor Juana Inés de la Cruz, *Yo, la peor de todas* (I, the worst of all), which was severely circumscribed by financial difficulties, one must recognize that the momentum of a new, redemocratized Argentine filmmaking is now very much a part of national cultural history.

This temporal circumscription provides the films with a privileged position not readily ascribable to other cultural genres. Of course, no claim can be made for the universal excellence of the several dozen films produced under the aegis of the redemocratization efforts, and a study more devoted to technical and artistic features than the present one might dwell at length on a recurring problem of symbolic pretentiousness and an ill-advised patina of Hollywood-ishness—allegedly part of the attempt to tap into international interest in Argentine and Latin American postdicta-

3. Schumann, *Historia del cine latinoamericano,* 35.

torship societies. These are some of the reasons why John King has been able to assert that, as a body, these films constitute an "imperfect cinema."[4] Yet from a strictly ideological frame of reference, the coincidence of this film production with the period of redemocratization provides it with a particular privilege as a record of the aspirations and limitations of that process. At the same time, one must recognize that the historicization of recent Argentine cinematography is, perhaps, what has limited its attractiveness to international audiences, which are likely to care little for the facts of Argentine history. The analyses herein, while centered on only a limited number of films—those that arguably represent the principal tendencies and recognized successes of their directors—have dealt with the interaction between cinematographic semiosis and the goals of redemocratization to analyze recent and long-range national history, to interpret the social and political forces at play during the dictatorship, and to project the collective and personal mentalities necessary for the shift in Argentine society that can impede the development of future tyrannies. No one can assume, protestations of Nunca más to the contrary, that the military will never come to power again in Argentina. Nor can anyone hope to provoke profound modifications in a country's deeply rooted social structures through a six-year politically based action program. But culture is a slowly evolving and immensely complex process. Because film is, after all, a recent but highly public cultural genre, it may be difficult to see its processes of ideological analysis and social impact from the sort of distanced perspective from which one views canonical genres like poetry or the theater. That is, it is all too easy to expect too much from, and to attribute too much to, a circumscribed production like the moviemaking examined in this study. Yet it can be only through the patient examination of this production that it will eventually be possible to ascertain its historical importance.

4. King and Torrents, eds., *The Garden of Forking Paths,* 93.

■ ■ ■ ■ ■   REFERENCES   ■ ■ ■ ■ ■

Acevedo, Zelmar. *Homosexualidad: hacia la destrucción de los mitos* (Buenos Aires: Ediciones del Ser, 1985), 118–19.

Aguinis, Marcos. *Mientras se consolida la democracia.* Buenos Aires: Fundación Demos; Fundación San Telmo, 1985.

Almoina Fidalgo, Helena. *Hacia una bibliografía en castellano del cine.* Mexico City: Universidad Nacional Autónoma de México/Secretaría de Educación Pública, 1988.

Armes, Roy. *Third World Film Making and the West.* Berkeley and Los Angeles: University of California Press, 1987.

Asís, Jorge. *Los reventados.* Buenos Aires: Editorial Sudamericana, 1977.

Avellaneda, Andrés. *Censura, autoritarismo y cultura: Argentina, 1960–1983.* Buenos Aires: Centro Editor de América Latina, 1986.

Barnard, Tim, ed. *Argentine Cinema.* Toronto: Nightwood Editions, 1986.

Barnouw, Erik. *Documentary: A History of the Non-Fiction Film.* Rev. ed. Oxford: Oxford University Press, 1983.

Beceyro, Raúl. *Ensayos sobre cine argentino.* Rosario, Argentina: Universidad Nacional del Litoral, Cuadernos de Extensión Universitaria, 1986.

Birri, Fernando. "Cinema and Underdevelopment." In *Twenty-five Years of the New Latin American Cinema,* edited by Michael Chanan, 9–12. London: British Film Institute, 1983.

Bordwell, David. *Narration in the Fiction Film.* Madison: University of Wisconsin Press, 1985.

Bortnik, Aída, and Luis Puenzo. *La historia oficial.* Buenos Aires: Ediciones de la Urraca, 1985.

Bossío, Jorge Alberto. *Los cafés de Buenos Aires.* Buenos Aires: Editorial Schapire, 1968.

Bottone, Mireya. *La literatura argentina y el cine.* Rosario, Argentina: Cuadernos del Instituto de Letras, Facultad de Filosofía y Letras, Universidad Nacional del Litoral, 1964.

Brownmiller, Susan. *Against Our Will: Men, Women, and Rape.* New York: Simon and Schuster, 1975.

Burns, E. Bradford. *Latin American Cinema: Film and History*. Los Angeles: UCLA Latin American Center, 1975.

Burton, Julianne. *The Social Documentary in Latin America*. Pittsburgh: University of Pittsburgh Press, 1990.

———, ed. *Cinema and Social Change in Latin America: Conversations with Filmmakers*. Austin: University of Texas Press, 1986.

Chanan, Michael, ed. *Twenty-five Years of the New Latin American Cinema*. London: British Film Institute, 1983.

Cine argentino. Buenos Aires: Ediciones Corregidor, 1976–[?].

Cine argentino: historia, documentación, filografía. Buenos Aires: Cine Libre, ca. 1983[?]–[?].

"El cine en América Latina." *Comunicación y cultura* 5 (1987).

Cine libre. Buenos Aires: Editorial Legasa, 1982–[?].

Les Cinémas de l'Amérique Latine. Paris: Lherminier, 1981.

Cook, David A. *A History of the Narrative Film*. London: W. W. Norton, 1981.

Cowles, Fleur. *Bloody Precedent: The Perón Story*. London: F. Muller, 1952.

De Lauretis, Teresa. *Alice Doesn't: Feminism, Semiotics, Cinema*. Bloomington: Indiana University Press, 1984.

"Dialogue on Film: Luis Puenzo." *American Film* 12 (1986): 15–18, 48.

Didion, Joan. "New York: Sentimental Journeys." *New York Review of Books* 38, nos. 1–2 (January 17, 1991): 45–56.

Dworkin, Andrea. *Intercourse*. New York: Free Press, 1987.

Dyer, Richard. *Now You See It: Studies on Lesbian and Gay Film*. London: Routledge, 1990.

———, ed. *Gays and Film*. London: British Film Institute, 1977.

Ellis, Jack C. *The Documentary Idea: A Critical History of English-Language Documentary Film and Video*. Englewood Cliffs, N.J.: Prentice Hall, 1989.

Ferreira, Carlos. *Por un cine libre*. Buenos Aires: Ediciones Corregidor, 1983.

Ford, Aníbal, Jorge B. Rivera, and Eduardo Romano. *Medios de comunicación y cultura popular*. Buenos Aires: Editorial Legasa, 1985.

Foster, David William. "Argentine Sociopolitical Commentary, the Malvinas Conflict, and Beyond: Rhetoricizing a National Experience." *Latin American Research Review* 22, no. 1 (1987): 7–34.

———. "Fiction and the Sociopolitical Text: Violence, the Body, and Cultural Responses in Argentine Literature in the Context of Military Tyranny." Manuscript in author's possession.

———. *Gay and Lesbian Themes in Latin American Writing*. Austin: University of Texas Press, 1991.

———. "Latin American Documentary Narrative." *PMLA* 99, no. 1 (1984): 41–55.

———. "Narrativa testimonial argentina durante los años del 'Proceso.'" In *Testimonio y literatura,* edited by René Jara and Hernán Vidal, 138–54. Minneapolis: Institute for the Study of Ideologies and Literature; Society for the Study of Contemporary Hispanic and Lusophone Revolutionary Literatures, 1986.

———. "Los parámetros de la narrativa argentina durante el 'Proceso de Reorganización Nacional.'" In *Ficción y política: la narrativa argentina durante el proceso militar,* edited by Beatriz Sarlo, 96–108. Buenos Aires: Alianza Editorial, and Minneapolis: Institute for the Study of Ideologies and Literature, 1987.

———. *Social Realism in Argentine Narrative.* North Carolina Studies in the Romance Languages and Literature. Chapel Hill: University of North Carolina, 1986.

Fusco, Coco. "The Tango of Esthetics and Politics: An Interview with Fernando Solanas." *Cineaste* 16, nos. 1–2 (1987–1988): 57–59.

Gabriel, Teshome H. *Third Cinema in the Third World: The Aesthetics of Liberation.* Ann Arbor: UMI Research Press, 1982.

Getino, Octavio. *Cine latinoamericano: economía y nuevas tecnologías audiovisuales.* Buenos Aires: Editorial Legasa, 1988.

Giussani, Pablo. *Montoneros, la soberbia armada.* 6th ed. Buenos Aires: Editorial Planeta/Sudamericana, 1986.

Hacia una Argentina posible. Buenos Aires: Fundación Bolsa de Comercio de Buenos Aires, 1984.

Historia del cine argentino. Buenos Aires: Centro Editor de América Latina, 1984.

Jameson, Fredric. "Modernism and Imperialism." In *Nationalism, Colonialism, and Literature,* 41–66. Minneapolis: University of Minnesota Press, 1990.

———. *Postmodernism; or, the Cultural Logic of Late Capitalism.* Durham: Duke University Press, 1990.

Jelin, Elizabeth. "Buenos Aires: Class Structure, Public Policy and the Urban Poor." In *Cities in Crisis: the Urban Challenge in the Americas,* edited by Matthew Edel and Ronald G. Hellman, 91–101. New York: Blinder Center for Western Hemisphere Studies, 1989.

Jelin, Elizabeth, and Pablo Vila. *Podría ser yo: los sectores populares urbanos en imagen y palabra.* Photographs by Alicia D'Amico. Buenos Aires: Cedes/Ediciones de la Flor, 1987.

King, John. "Assailing the Heights of Macho Pictures: Women Filmmakers in Contemporary Argentina." In *Knives and Angels: Women Writers in Latin America,* edited by Susan Bassnett, 158–70. London: Zed Books, 1990.

King, John, and Nissa Torrents, eds. *The Garden of Forking Paths: Argentine Cinema.* London: British Film Institute, 1988.

Kovadloff, Santiago. "Los chicos y la dictadura." In *Argentina, oscuro país: ensayos sobre un tiempo de quebranto,* 39–47. Buenos Aires: Torres Agüero Editores, 1983.

Laclau, Ernesto. "Fascismo e ideología." In *Política e ideología en la teoría marxista: capitalismo, fascismo, populismo,* 89–164. 3d ed. Madrid: Siglo XXI de España Editores, 1986.

Landi, Oscar. "Campo cultural y democratización en Argentina *Políticas culturales en América Latina,* edited by Néstor García Canclini, 145–73. Mexico City: Grijalbo, 1987.

López, Daniel, comp. *Catálogo del nuevo cine argentino, 1984–1986.* Buenos Aires: Instituto Nacional de Cinematografía, 1987.

————, comp. *Catálogo del nuevo cine argentino, 1987–1988.* Buenos Aires: Instituto Nacional de Cinematografía, 1989.

Lotersztein, Salomon. "Cine argentino: participación, temática y contribución judías—reflexiones." In *Ensayos sobre judaísmo latinoamericano,* 339–49. Buenos Aires: Milá, 1990.

Lotman, Jurij. *Semiotics of Cinema.* Translated from the Russian, and with a foreword, by Mark E. Suino. Ann Arbor: Michigan Slavic Series, 1976.

Lynch, John. *Argentine Dictator: Juan Manuel de Rosas, 1829–1852.* Oxford, England: Clarendon Press, 1981.

Magrini, César. *Cine argentino contemporáneo.* Buenos Aires: Revista Cultura/Colección Union Carbide, 1985.

Mahieu, Agustín. *Breve historia del cine nacional.* Buenos Aires: Alzamor Editores, 1974.

Martín, Jorge Abel. *Una cierta mirada.* Buenos Aires: Corregidor, 1985.

Martínez Torres, Augusto, and Manuel Pérez Estremera. "Introducción a la historia del cine argentino." *Cuadernos hispanoamericanos* 262 (1972): 38–53.

Metz, Christian. *Film Language: A Semiotics of the Cinema.* Translated by Michael Taylor. New York: Oxford University Press, 1974.

Mignogna, Eduardo. *Evita: quien quiera oír, que oiga.* Buenos Aires: Editorial Legasa, 1984.

Muraro, Heriberto, and José G. Cantor Magnani. "La influencia transnacional en el cine argentino." *Comunicación y cultura* 5 (1987): 19–69.

Nunca más: informe de la Comisión Nacional sobre la Desaparición de Personas. Buenos Aires: EUDEBA, 1984. Also in English as *Nunca más: The Report of the Argentine National Commission on the Disappeared.* Introduction by Ronald Dworkin. New York: Farrar Straus Giroux, in association with Index on Censorship, London, 1986.

Peralta-Ramos, Mónica, and Carlos H. Waisman, eds. *From Military Rule to Liberal Democracy in Argentina*. Boulder, Colo.: Westview, 1987.

Petit de Murat, Ulyses. *Este cine argentino*. Buenos Aires: Ediciones del Carro de Tespis, 1959.

Reati, Fernando. "Argentine Political Violence and Artistic Representation in Films of the 1980's." *Latin American Literary Review* 34 (1989): 24-39.

Rich, B. Ruby. "An/Other View of New Latin American Cinema." *Iris: revue de théorie de l'image et du son* 13 (1991): 5-28.

Rodowick, D. N. *The Crisis of Political Modernism: Criticism and Ideology in Contemporary Film Theory*. Urbana: University of Illinois Press, 1988.

————. *The Difficulty of Difference: Psychoanalysis, Sexual Difference, and Film Theory*. New York: Routledge, 1991.

Ross, Andrew. *No Respect: Intellectuals and Popular Culture*. New York: Routledge, 1989.

Russo, Vito. *The Celluloid Closet: Homosexuality in the Movies*. Rev. ed. New York: Harper & Row, 1987.

Sarlo, Beatriz, ed. *Ficción y política: la narrativa argentina durante el proceso militar*. Buenos Aires: Alianza Editorial, and Minneapolis: Institute for the Study of Ideologies and Literature, 1987.

Schnitman, Jorge A. *Film Industries in Latin America: Dependency and Development*. Norwood, N.J.: Ablex, 1984.

Schrader, Leonard. *Kiss of the Spider Woman: The Screenplay*. Boston: Faber and Faber, 1987.

Schumann, Peter B. *Historia del cine latinoamericano*. Translated from the German by Oscar Zambrano. Buenos Aires: Editorial Legasa, 1987.

Sedgwick, Eve Kosofsky. *Epistemology of the Closet*. Berkeley and Los Angeles: University of California Press, 1991.

Semana de literatura y cine argentinos. Mendoza, Argentina: Universidad Nacional de Cuyo, Facultad de Filosofía y Letras, 1972.

Simpson, John, and Jana Bennett. *The Disappeared: Voices from a Secret War*. London: Robson Books, 1985.

Solanas, Fernando E., and Octavio Getino. *Cine, cultura y descolonización*. Buenos Aires: Siglo XXI Editores, 1973.

Spivak, Gayatri Chakravorty. "Can the Subaltern Speak?" In *Marxism and the Interpretation of Culture,* edited by Cary Nelson and Lawrence Grossberg, 271-313. Urbana: University of Illinois Press, 1988.

Suvin, Darko. *Metamorphoses of Science Fiction: On the Poetics and History of a Literary Genre.* New Haven: Yale University Press, 1979.

——.*Positions and Presuppositions in Science Fiction.* Kent, Ohio: Kent State University Press, 1988.

Taylor, Julie M. *Eva Perón: The Myths of a Woman.* Chicago: University of Chicago Press, 1979.

Timerman, Jacobo. *Preso sin nombre, celda sin número.* Barcelona: El Cid Editor, 1980. Cover title: *El caso Camps, punto inicial.* Also in English as *Prisoner without a Name, Cell without a Number.* Translated from the Spanish by Toby Talbot. New York: Knopf/Random House, 1981.

Torre, Javier, and Adriana Zaffaroni. "Argentina: Its Culture during the Repression and during the Transition." In *The Redemocratization of Argentine Culture, 1983 and Beyond,* edited by David William Foster, 11–21. Tempe: Arizona State University, Center for Latin American Studies, 1989.

Torrents, Nissa. "One Woman's Cinema: Interview with María Luisa Bemberg." In *Knives and Angels: Women Writers in Latin America,* edited by Susan Bassnett, 171–75. London: Zed Books, 1990.

Vezzetti, Hugo. *La locura en la Argentina.* Buenos Aires: Folio Ediciones, 1983.

Viñas, David. *Indios, ejército y frontera.* Mexico City: Siglo XXI Editores, 1982.

——. *¿Qué es el fascismo en Latinoamérica?* Barcelona: Editorial de la Gaya Ciencia, 1977.

Vizoso Gorostiaga, Manuel. *Camila O'Gorman y su época.* Santa Fe, Argentina: n.p., 1943.

Weisbrot, Robert. *The Jews of Argentina: From the Inquisition to Perón.* Philadelphia: Jewish Publication Society of America, 1979.

Wyver, John. *The Moving Image: An International History of Film, Television, and Video.* Oxford, England: Basil Blackwell, 1989.

INDEX